CRACKING THE MACHINE LEARNING INTERVIEW

225 Machine Learning Interview Questions with Solutions

Nitin Suri

CRACKING THE MACHINE LEARNING INTERVIEW

Acknowledgements

This book would not exist if it weren't for my big brother, **Heemanshu Suri**. I shall forever be indebted to him for providing his profound insight into the field of Machine Learning. It is his proficiency in this domain, which lent to the inception of this project.

To elaborate a little on his background, Heemanshu has worked for some of the major tech companies as well as Silicon Valley Startups in the Software Engineering and Data Science fields and is presently working for Microsoft in the Artificial Intelligence and Data Infrastructure Group. In addition, he founded MyyUtopia in January 2017, an interest-based hyper-local social networking platform which makes use of an innovative Machine Learning technique to help users connect with like-minded people nearby and find local groups and events of their interests. At present, MyyUtopia is available on Google Play Store serving roughly 10,000 users.

The idea behind writing this book was conceived when he was still a graduate student in Computer Sciences at the University of Wisconsin-Madison, USA, where he spent the majority of his time learning Artificial Intelligence and Machine Learning in depth. Most of the problems and their solutions, presented in this book, are a result of hours and hours of brainstorming sessions with him.

CRACKING THE MACHINE LEARNING INTERVIEW is a result of his experiences along with his wide-ranging interactions with other interviewers from various Silicon Valley companies ranging from early-stage startups to mid-growth companies to tech giants such as Google and Facebook. I dedicate this book to him. Thank you Big B!

Another name which deserves a very special acknowledgement is my friend, **Vasundhara**. From reading early drafts to advising me on the structure of the book to making sure that it was written in a manner that was coherent, organised and engaging at the same time, her role has been pivotal in the drafting of this book. Thank you.

To **Nikhil Suri**, for his patience in reading through various preliminary versions of this book, and his vital suggestions. Thank you brother for never saying no to my numerous feedback requests and providing all the constructive criticism.

Finally, I would like to express my sincere gratitude to my family, friends, and everyone who motivated me throughout. Thanks for the support, the honest feedback, and for everything else that has helped to make this book possible in its current form.

This page intentionally left blank

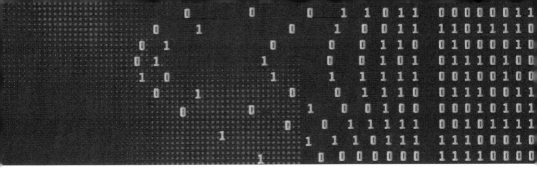

Table of Contents

I	Introduction	9
II	Why Machine Learning	11
III	Machine Learning Workflow	12
IV	How this book is organized	14
5	General Machine Learning Questions	15
6	Supervised Learning	35

6.1	**Classification**	**35**
	6.1.1 Decision Trees	42
	6.1.2 Ensembles	47
	6.1.3 K-Nearest Neighbors	50
	6.1.4 Logistic Regression	54
	6.1.5 Support Vector Machines	57
	6.1.6 Artificial Neural Networks	63
6.2	**Regression**	**72**

| 6.3 | Regularization | 78 |

7	Unsupervised Learning	83
7.1	Clustering	84
7.2	Dimensionality Reduction	88

| 8 | Data Preprocessing . . . . | 95 |

| 9 | Model Evaluation . . . . | 99 |

| 10 | Natural Language Processing . . . . | 105 |

| 11 | Real World Problems . . . . | 109 |

| XII | Glossary . . . . | 111 |

| XIII | About The Author . . . . | 114 |

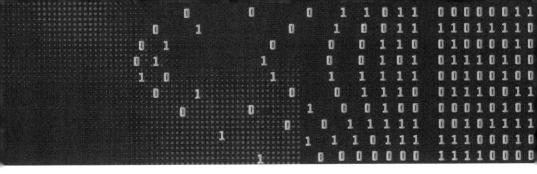

I. Introduction

CRACKING THE MACHINE LEARNING INTERVIEW is a result of my brother, Heemanshu Suri, and my own experiences along with our interactions with other interviewers from various Silicon Valley companies ranging from early-stage startups to tech giants such as Google and Facebook.

Quite often both the students and working professionals seem clueless about how and from where to prepare for Data Science or Machine Learning interviews. I can still recall the time when I was preparing for a job in this field and was left wanting for a complete book which could provide a comprehensive learning platform to prepare from. My peers across the world, on both sides of the interview table, have also acknowledged the presence of such a gap.

In this book, I have tried to mitigate such struggles and attempted to create an extensive list of Machine Learning (ML) topics one could face in an interview. This book is composed and structured in a manner that can be used by an array of individuals from a complete beginner to people with intermediate to advanced level of expertise in ML. Enclosed in this book are 225 of the best interview problems and their solutions, selected from the mines of hundreds and thousands of potential problems.

An important point to note here is that the interviews for Machine Learning jobs are quite different from the traditional software development interviews. In an ML interview, the emphasis is laid more on your understanding of the type of data you are dealing with, the end results you are interested in, such as accuracy or performance, and the kind of learning algorithm you prefer instead of actually coding up the solution. Unlike typical coding questions that would usually result in a single correct answer, it is generally very hard to find "the single most optimal solution" for your Machine Learning problem. You would need to keep improving your algorithm's accuracy iteratively.

Who is this book for?

This book is for you if you are either preparing for an interview, planning to move into this field in future, brushing up your Machine Learning skills or just want to get an in-depth overview of the field. This book provides the most important and frequently asked questions along with their solutions, with each chapter as a self-contained Machine Learning topic.

Who is this book NOT for?

This book is not for you if you are looking for an in-depth study of Artificial Intelligence or Machine Learning. The objective of this book is not to discuss the ongoing research or challenges in this industry or serve as a substitute for a course book.

If you follow this book diligently, you would be better equipped to face any Machine Learning interview. Whether you are a beginner or an intermediate level expert in ML, this book has enough juice for you. I hope that this book serves as an enjoyable preparation for Machine Learning.

Final piece of advice

Artificial Intelligence, Machine Learning, and Big Data are among the hot topics in the tech industry right now and the demand for the jobs in these fields has been on a continuous rise. This is a golden opportunity and now is the perfect time to dive into this field, if you haven't already. The jobs and the corresponding salaries offered to a Machine Learning expert or a Data Scientist are astonishing right now. My advice for you is to take advantage of this opportunity and do not delay, or you would be left behind! So let's get started on preparing you well for Cracking The Machine Learning Interview RIGHT NOW!

I wish you all the very best for your future endeavors!
- Nitin Suri

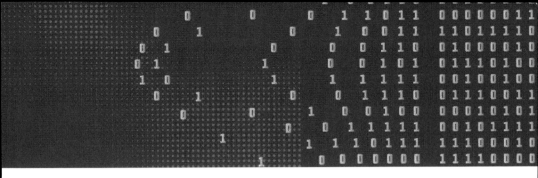

II. Why Machine Learning

"A breakthrough in machine learning would be worth ten Microsofts." -Bill Gates

Looking at the past trends, the world data is expected to double every two years with the cost of data storage declining at roughly the same rate. In order to extract the information from this exponentially increasing data, the need for better Machine Learning techniques is at an all-time high.

Machine Learning is perhaps one of the hottest fields in the world right now, not just in Silicon Valley. You can see the applications of Machine Learning probably everywhere around you, for instance in gadgets such as Amazon Echo and Google Home, personalized ads shown on Facebook, Video recommendations on Netflix and Youtube, Product recommendations on e-commerce platforms such as Amazon and Flipkart.

Every industry, every company is using Artificial Intelligence and Machine Learning in one way or another. For any company wanting to gauge the reach of their business and products, using Machine Learning techniques is the only scalable approach in the long term. The major use cases of Machine Learning lies in analyzing Big Data, creating Predictive Models and Deep Insights.

It is not surprising that the demand for Data Scientists and Machine Learning engineers is more than ever before. And, I believe that it is extremely crucial to keep yourself up to date on the latest research and developments in this field. Be it automation, personalization, cognitive services or predictive analytics, Machine Learning is going to be the center point of all such fields.

"Machine learning and deep learning will create a new set of hot jobs in the next 5 years." -Dave Waters

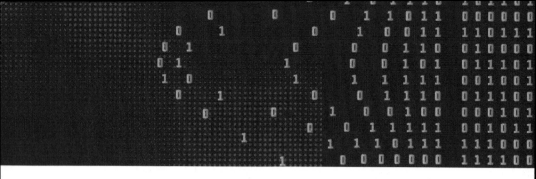

III. Machine Learning Workflow

Any company which operates in the Big Data Analytics and/or Machine Learning world, would, at some point, be involved in designing the Data Processing and Machine Learning pipeline to support it. Various factors affect a company's choice of using a particular Machine Learning workflow. The type and amount of data supplied to the pipeline, speed with which the data is being supplied, available storage system, the extent to which preprocessing is needed to clean the data, the goal of the overall project, any time bounds on the Machine Learning model for prediction, threshold for model's accuracy are just a few of the numerous details which need to be considered in order to design a specific workflow.

However, all of these factors can be broadly grouped into five major stages, which are common to any workflow. These stages differ from company to company with respect to their implementation details.

Figure III.1: Typical Machine Learning Workflow

Let's discuss each of the stages mentioned in Figure III.1 in detail.

Step 1. Data Gathering
The first step in any workflow is collecting the data. Data is nothing but the list of observations or examples which are fed to the system. The system can accumulate it from either a single source or multiple data stores.

Step 2. Data Cleaning
Quite often, real-world data is not perfect. It contains missing values, corrupt or inaccurate observations. The Data Cleaning step handles such irregularities by either formatting those entries suitably or removing them from the set if needed.

Step 3. Feature Extraction
Once you have a clean dataset, you need to transform it into a new set of features to remove noise and redundant information from the input data. This step also involves Feature Engineering, in which you use the domain knowledge of the data to transform it into the features which would improve the accuracy of your Machine Learning model.

Step 4. Model Training
This is the main step in which the Machine Learning model is actually built by using a particular algorithm and input training data from the previous step. Depending upon the size of the data, the type of algorithm used and/or the hardware on which it is run, this step can take anywhere from few minutes to hours to learn the model.

Step 5. Prediction
The final step of the pipeline is to evaluate the performance of the model you just trained. The company could have its own metric to measure the performance. If the performance of the model does not meet the acceptance criteria, then Step 4 is repeated again with the updated information to re-train the model. Steps 4 and 5 often have to be repeated back and forth multiple times before a good enough model can be trained. Finally, the model is deployed to the production.

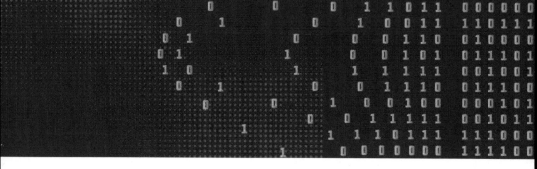

IV. How this book is organized

This book covers the major areas of Machine Learning asked in the job interviews. It consists of the following chapters:

- Chapter 5. General Machine Learning Questions

- Chapter 6. Supervised Learning

- Chapter 7. Unsupervised Learning

- Chapter 8. Data Preprocessing

- Chapter 9. Model Evaluation

- Chapter 10. Natural Language Processing

- Chapter 11. Real World Problems

Each chapter in this book is a self-contained lesson for you to work through. Sections and subsections within each chapter are organized as a set of questions and answers. We have also provided python code snippets using Scikit-Learn for some of our questions. You can find them on github as well:
https://github.com/crackingthemachinelearninginterview/Cracking-The-Machine-Learning-Interview

Chapter 11 sets the interviewer's expectations in the system design problems and questions asked on the real world scenarios. Since the system design problems could be open-ended, hence, we have provided a list of key points to consider and the general order of steps in which to think about while answering such questions.

5. General Machine Learning Questions

This chapter introduces you to the field of Machine Learning and gives an idea of how it fits within the Artificial Intelligence domain. In this chapter, we will cover questions from different areas of Machine Learning. We will delve deeper into these areas and discuss them in depth in the next few chapters.

This chapter provides a comprehensive overview of the general questions put forth in the interviews. After completing this chapter, you would achieve a fairly decent understanding of the overall Machine Learning process.

Alright, enough of talking. Let's start preparing!

1 **Define Machine Learning. How is it different from Artificial Intelligence?**
   Machine Learning is a subset of Artificial Intelligence that aims at making systems learn automatically from the data provided and improve their learnings over time without being explicitly programmed.

   Artificial Intelligence (AI) is the broader concept of machines being able to carry out tasks in a way that could be considered as smart. The machines not necessarily learn from the data but may exhibit *intelligence* in performing certain tasks that mimic the characteristic of human intelligence.

   Above and beyond Machine Learning, AI includes Self Driving Cars, Natural Language Processing (NLP), Knowledge Representation etc. As can be seen in Figure 5.1, Deep learning is a subset of Machine Learning which itself is a subset of the overall Artificial Intelligence concept.

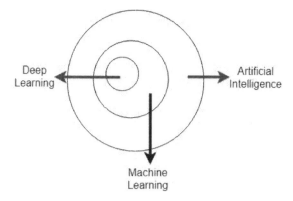

Figure 5.1: Artificial Intelligence Set

2 How would you differentiate a Machine Learning algorithm from other algorithms?

A Machine Learning algorithm is an application that can learn from the data without relying on the explicit instructions to follow. On the contrary, a traditional algorithm is a process or set of rules to be followed especially by a computer, which does not learn anything on its own.

For instance, let us say that you want to compute the sum of 2 numbers. A traditional algorithm would implement a sum function which is explicitly programmed to take the input numbers and return their sum. However, a Machine Learning algorithm would take as input the sample (training) dataset with the numbers and their corresponding sum and would learn the pattern automatically such that given a new pair of numbers (test data), it would return their sum itself without being explicitly programmed to do so.

```
# Let's train a simple Scikit-Learn Linear model that
# returns the sum of two numbers
from sklearn import linear_model
import numpy as np

# First, create our training (input) dataset.
# The input_data has 2 input integers and
# the input_sum is the resulting sum of them.
input_data = np.random.randint(50, size=(20, 2))
input_sum = np.zeros(len(input_data))
for row in range(len(input_data)):
    input_sum[row] = input_data[row][0] + input_data[row][1]

# Now, we will build a simple Linear Regression model
# which trains on this dataset.
linear_regression_model = linear_model.LinearRegression(
    fit_intercept=False)
linear_regression_model.fit(input_data, input_sum)

# Once, the model is trained, let's see what it
# predicts for the new data.
predicted_sum = linear_regression_model.predict([[60, 24]])
```

```
print("Predicted sum of 60 and 24 is " + str(predicted_sum))

# To give you an insight into this model,
# it predicts the output using the following equation:
# output = <coefficient for 1st number> * < 1st number> +
#          <coefficient for 2nd number> * < 2nd number>

# Now, our model should have 1, 1 as the coefficients
# which means it figured out that for 2 inout integers,
# it has to return their sum
print("Coefficients of both the inputs are " +
      str(linear_regression_model.coef_))

# This is, of course, very basic stuff,
# but I hope you get the idea.
```

3 **What do you understand by Deep Learning and what are some of the main characteristics that distinguish it from traditional Machine Learning?**

As shown in Figure 5.1, Deep learning is a subset of the broader Machine Learning concept, and is inspired by the function and the structure of the human brain.

Deep Learning is based on learning the data representation itself.

(a) The most important difference between Deep Learning and traditional Machine Learning is the performance of Deep Learning as the scale of data increases. Deep Learning algorithms need a large amount of data to understand it perfectly, which is why they do not perform well when given a small dataset.

(b) Deep Learning algorithms try to learn the high-level features (important and relevant characteristics of the dataset) on their own, as opposed to the traditional Machine Learning algorithms, which require a manual input of the feature set.

(c) Deep Learning algorithms rely heavily on GPU and generally need high-end machines to train. This is because they perform a large number of multiplications and other operations which could be highly parallelized in GPUs. A Deep Neural Network consists of many hidden layers with hundreds of neurons in each layer and each layer performs the same computation. Using a high-end machine and/or GPU would drastically speed up the overall processing by executing each layer's computation in parallel.

4 **What is the difference between Data Mining and Machine Learning?**

Machine Learning is a branch of Artificial Intelligence which aims at making systems learn automatically from the data provided and improve their learning over time without being explicitly programmed.

Data Mining, on the other hand, focuses on analyzing the data and extracting knowledge and/or unknown interesting patterns from it. The goal is to understand the patterns in the data in order to explain some phenomenon and not to develop a sophisticated model which can predict the outcomes for the unknown/new data.

For instance, you can use Data Mining on the existing data to understand your company's sales trends and then build a Machine Learning Model to learn from that data, find the correlations and adapt for the new data.

5 What is Inductive Machine Learning?

Inductive Machine Learning involves the process of learning by examples, where a system tries to induce a general rule from a set of observed instances. The classic Machine Learning approach follows the paradigm of induction and deduction.

Inductive Machine Learning is nothing but the inductive step in which you learn the model from the given dataset. Similarly, the deductive step is the one in which the learned model is used to predict the outcome of the test dataset.

6 Pick an algorithm you like and walk me through the math and then the implementation of it, in pseudo-code.

Here, you can talk about any particular algorithm that you have worked on and/or feel comfortable discussing.

7 Do you know any tools for running a Machine Learning algorithm in parallel?

Some of the tools, software or hardware, used to execute the Machine Learning algorithms in parallel include Matlab Parfor, GPUs, MapReduce, Spark, Graphlab, Giraph, Vowpal, Parameter Server etc.

8 What tools and environments have you used to train and evaluate the Machine Learning models?

You can talk about your prior experiences. We have an entire chapter on Model Evaluation (Chapter 9) where we would cover all the important questions related to it.

9 Do you have any prior experience with Spark or big data tools for Machine Learning?

Again, you can talk about your prior experiences here.

10 What are the different Machine Learning approaches?

The different types of techniques in Machine Learning are:

    (a) **Supervised Learning** where the output variable (the one you want to predict) is labeled in the training dataset (data used to build the Machine Learning model). Techniques include Decision Trees, Random Forests, Support Vector Machines, Bayesian Classifier etc. For instance, predicting whether a given email is SPAM or not, given sample emails with the labels whether they are SPAM or not, falls within Supervised learning.

    (b) **Unsupervised Learning** where the training dataset does not contain the output variable. The objective is to group the similar data together instead of predicting any specific value. Clustering, Dimensionality Reduction and

Anomaly Detection are some of the Unsupervised Learning techniques. For instance, grouping the customers based on their purchasing pattern.

(c) **Semi-supervised Learning**: This technique falls in between Supervised and Unsupervised Learning because it has a small amount of labeled data with a relatively large amount of unlabeled data. You can find its applications in problems such as Web Content Classification, and Speech Recognition, where it is very hard to get labeled data but you can easily get lots of unlabeled data.

(d) **Reinforcement Learning**: Unlike traditional Machine Learning techniques, Reinforcement Learning focuses on finding a balance between Exploration (of unknown new territory) and Exploitation (of current knowledge). It monitors the response of the actions taken through trial and error and measures the response against a reward. The goal is to take such actions for the new data so that the long-term reward is maximized. Let's say that you are in an unknown terrain, and each time you step on a rock, you get negative reward whereas each time you find a coin, you get a positive reward. In traditional Machine Learning, at each step, you would greedily take such an action whose immediate reward is maximum even though there might be another path for which the overall reward is more. In Reinforcement Learning, after every few steps, you take a less greedy step to explore the full terrain. After much exploration and exploitation, you would know the best way to walk through the terrain so as to maximize your total reward.

11 How would you differentiate between Supervised and Unsupervised Learning?
Supervised Learning is where you have both the input variable x and the output variable y and you use an algorithm to learn the mapping function from x to y and predict the output of the new data. Supervised Learning can further be classified as a Classification or a Regression technique.

Unsupervised Learning, on the other hand, is where you only have the input variable x but no corresponding output variable y. The goal in Unsupervised Learning is to model the underlying structure and distribution of the data. Unsupervised Learning techniques include Clustering, Anomaly Detection, and Dimensionality Reduction.

12 What are the different stages to learn the hypotheses or models in Machine Learning?
A hypothesis is a function that is (very close to) the true function which maps the input to the output. The goal is to find such a hypothesis which can learn the true function as efficiently as possible. Following are the three main stages of learning a model:

(a) **Model building**: Learning from the training dataset and building a Machine Learning model using it.

(b) **Model testing**: Testing the learned model using the test dataset.

(c) **Applying the model**: Model building and testing are performed iteratively until the learned model reaches the desired accuracy. Once the model is finalized, it is applied to the new data.

```
# Let's use Support Vector Machine for our question.
from sklearn.svm import SVC
from sklearn import datasets
from sklearn.model_selection import train_test_split
from sklearn.metrics import classification_report

# In this example, we will use the standard iris dataset
iris = datasets.load_iris()

# Here, we will split it into training and
# test dataset (90-10 ratio).
X_train, X_test, y_train, y_test = train_test_split(iris.data
    , iris.target, test_size=0.10)

# Model building is initializing a Model with
# the correct set of parameters
# and fitting our training dataset.
model = SVC(kernel='linear')
model.fit(X_train, y_train)

# Model testing is predicting the values for test dataset
y_predicted = model.predict(X_test)
print(classification_report(y_test, y_predicted))

# Based on the model's metrics, you can either deploy
# your model or re-train it.
```

13 What is the difference between Causation and Correlation?

Causation is a relationship between two variables such that one of them is caused by the occurrence of the other.

Correlation, on the other hand, is a relationship observed between two variables which are related to each other but not caused by one another.

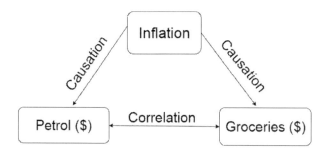

Figure 5.2: Causation vs Correlation

In Figure 5.2, you can see that *inflation* causes the price fluctuations in *petrol* and *groceries* so, *inflation* has a causation relationship with both of them. Between *petrol* and *groceries*, there is a correlation that both of them can increase or decrease due to the changes in *inflation*, but neither of them causes or impacts the other one.

14 What is the difference between Online and Offline (Batch) learning?
The major difference is that in case of Online learning, the data becomes available in real-time in a sequential manner, one example at a time, whereas in Offline learning, the complete dataset is statically available. An example of Online learning is a Real-Time recommendation system on amazon.com where Amazon learns from each purchase you make and recommends you similar products.

Each one has its own advantages and disadvantages. Online learning is time critical so you may not be able to use all the data to train your model whereas with offline learning, you won't be able to learn in real-time. Quite often, companies use a hybrid approach in which they train the models both online and offline. They would learn a model offline from the static data to interpret global patterns and then incorporate the real-time data for online learning.

For instance, Twitter could learn a model offline to analyze the sentiments on a global scale. And if an event is happening at a particular place, it could use an online learning model on top of the already learned model to interpret real-time sentiments of the event.

15 Differentiate between Classification and Regression.
Classification is a kind of Supervised Learning technique where the output label is discrete or categorical. Regression, on the other hand, is a Supervised Learning technique which is used to predict continuous or real-valued variables.

For instance, predicting stock price is a Regression problem because the stock price is a continuous variable which can take any real-value whereas predicting whether the email is spam or not is a Classification problem because in this case, the output is discrete and has only two possible values, yes or no.

16 Define Sampling. Why do we need it?
Sampling is a process of choosing a subset from a target population which would serve as its representative. We use the data from the sample to understand the pattern in the population as a whole. Sampling is necessary because often we can not gather or process the complete data within a reasonable time. There are many ways to perform sampling. Some of the most commonly used techniques are Random Sampling, Stratified Sampling, and Clustering Sampling.

17 What is stratified sampling?
Stratified sampling is a probability sampling technique wherein the entire population is divided into different subgroups called strata, and then a probability sample is drawn proportionally from each stratum.

For instance, in case of a binary classification, if the ratio of positive and negative labeled data was 9:1, then in stratified sampling, you would randomly select subsample from each of the positive and negative labeled dataset such that after sampling, their ratio is still 9:1.

Stratified sampling has several advantages over simple random sampling. For example, using stratified sampling, it may be possible to increase the precision with the same sample size or to reduce the sample size required to achieve the same precision.

18 Define Confidence interval.

A confidence interval is an interval estimate which is likely to include an unknown population parameter, the estimated range being calculated from the given sample dataset. It simply means the range of values for which you are completely sure that the true value of your variable would lie in.

19 What do you mean by i.i.d. assumption?

We often assume that the instances in the training dataset are independent and identically distributed (i.i.d.), i.e, they are mutually independent of each other and follow the same probability distribution. It means that the order in which the training instances are supplied should not affect your model and that the instances are not related to each other. If the instances do not follow an identical distribution, it would be fairly difficult to interpret the data.

20 Why do we call it GLM (Generalized Linear Model) when it is clearly non-linear?

The Generalized Linear Model (GLM) is a generalization of ordinary linear regression in which the response variables have error distribution models other than a normal distribution. The "linear" component in GLM means that the predictor is a linear combination of the parameters, and it is related to the response variable via a link function.

Let us assume that "Y" is the response variable and "X" is the input independent variable. Then,

$$E(\mathbf{Y}) = g^{-1}(\mathbf{X}\beta), \tag{5.1}$$

where E(Y) is the expected value of Y, $X\beta$ is the linear predictor, a linear combination of unknown parameters β and g is the link function.

21 Define Conditional Probability.

Conditional Probability is a measure of the probability of one event, given that another event has occurred. Let's say that you have 2 events, A and B. Then, the conditional probability of A, given B has already occurred, is given as:

$$P(A|B) = \frac{P(A \cap B)}{P(B)}, \tag{5.2}$$

where $\cap$ stands for intersection. So, the conditional probability is the joint probability of both the events divided by the probability of event B.

22 Are you familiar with Bayes Theorem? Can you tell me why is it useful?

Bayes Theorem is used to describe the probability of an event, based on the prior knowledge of other events related to it. For example, the probability of a person having a particular disease would be based on the symptoms shown.

Bayes Theorem can be mathematically formulated as:

$$P(A \mid B) = \frac{P(B \mid A)P(A)}{P(B)}, \tag{5.3}$$

where A and B are the events and $P(B) \neq 0$. Most of the times, we want $P(A \mid B)$ but we know $P(B \mid A)$. Bayes Theorem is extremely useful in these scenarios, as you can use it to predict $P(A \mid B)$ using the above equation.

For instance, let us say that you want to find the probability of a person suffering from liver disease given that he is an alcoholic. Now finding this directly is hard but you can have records of a person being an alcoholic, given that he is suffering from liver disease.

Let A be the event that the person has a liver disease and B be the event that he is an alcoholic. You want to find $P(A \mid B)$, but it is easier to find $P(B \mid A)$ since it is more common. This is where you can make use of the Bayes Theorem to achieve the desired result.

23 How can you get an unbiased estimate of the accuracy of the learned model?

Divide the input dataset into training and test datasets. Build the model using the training dataset and measure its accuracy on the test dataset. For better results, you can use Cross-validation to run multiple iterations of partitioning the dataset into the training and test datasets, analyze the accuracy of the learned model in each iteration and finally use the best model from the learned models.

Evaluating the model's performance with the training dataset is not a good measure because it can easily generate overfitted models which fit well on the given training dataset but do not show similar accuracy on the test dataset. Remember, the goal is to learn a model which can perform well on the new dataset.

You can also split the training set into training and validation set and use the validation dataset to prevent the model from overfitting the training dataset.

24 How would you handle the scenario where your dataset has missing or dirty (garbled) values?

These kind of situations are very common in real life. Sometimes, the data is missing or empty. And sometimes, it can have some unexpected values such as special characters while performing data transformations or saving/fetching the data from the client/server. Another case could be when you expect an ASCII string but receive a Unicode string which may result in garbled data in your string.

You can either drop those rows or columns or replace the missing/garbled values with other values such as the mean value of that column or the most occurring value etc. The latter case is generally known as "Parameter Estimation". Expectation Maximization (EM) is one of the algorithms used for the same. It is an iterative method to find the maximum likelihood or maximum a posteriori (MAP) estimates of the parameters in statistical models.

25 What is EM algorithm?

Expectation Maximization (EM) is an iterative method to find maximum likelihood or maximum a posteriori (MAP) estimates of the parameters in statistical models. It is an iterative process, repeated until convergence. There are 2 steps involved in the EM algorithm:

Expectation (E) step: Compute the Expectation over missing values using the current model.

Maximization (M) step: Given the Expectations from the previous step, compute the maximum a posterior probability (MAP) estimates of the parameters.

For instance, consider a scenario where you have the following three events:

(a) Event B that a burglary has happened in a house.

(b) Event A that the alarm was raised in case of a burglary.

(c) Event M that a message was sent to the house owner about the alarm.

The structure of these events would be like:

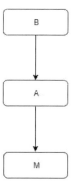

Figure 5.3: Events structure

In Figure 5.3, you can see that event M is dependent on A and A is dependent on B. Now let's suppose that you are given the following initial Bayes Network with the probability of event B and the conditional probabilities of events A and M:

P(B)
0.2

B	P(A)
t (true)	0.9
f (false)	0.1

A	P(M)
t	0.8
f	0.2

The above network tells us that the probability of burglary happening is 0.2, the probability of alarm being raised, given that the burglary happened, is 0.9 and so on. Let the training dataset be:

B	A	M
f	?	t
t	?	f

In the training dataset, the values of A are missing. First, E step - You need to calculate the Expectation of A for all the missing instances.

$$P(A = t \mid B = f, M = t) = \frac{P(B = f) * P(A = t \mid B = f) * P(M = t \mid A = t)}{P(B = f, M = t)}$$

$$= \frac{P(B = f) * P(A = t \mid B = f) * P(M = t \mid A = t)}{P(B = f, A = t, M = t) + P(B = f, A = f, M = t)}$$

$$= \frac{0.8 * 0.1 * 0.8}{0.8 * 0.1 * 0.8 + 0.8 * 0.9 * 0.2} = 0.308$$

$$P(A = t \mid B = t, M = f) = \frac{P(B = t) * P(A = t \mid B = t) * P(M = f \mid A = t)}{P(B = t, M = f)}$$

$$= \frac{P(B = t) * P(A = t \mid B = t) * P(M = f \mid A = t)}{P(B = t, A = t, M = f) + P(B = t, A = f, M = f)}$$

$$= \frac{0.2 * 0.9 * 0.2}{0.2 * 0.9 * 0.2 + 0.2 * 0.1 * 0.8} = 0.692$$

Updating the training set with these values, you get:

B	A	M
f	t = 0.308	t
f	f = 0.692	t
t	t = 0.692	f
t	f = 0.308	f

Now, you need to perform the M step, i.e, re-estimate the probabilities using the updated Expected counts.

For example,

$$P(A = t \mid B = t) = \frac{\text{Expected number of events where A = t and B = t}}{\text{Expected number of events where B = t}}$$

$$= \frac{P(A = t, B = t)}{P(B = t)}$$

$$= \frac{0.692}{0.692 + 0.308} \text{ (from the updated training set)} = 0.692$$

$$P(A = t \mid B = f) = \frac{0.308}{0.308 + 0.692} = 0.308$$

Similarly, for M: $P(M = t \mid A = t) = 0.308/(0.308 + 0.692) = 0.308$

$P(M = t \mid A = f) = 0.692/(0.692 + 0.308) = 0.692$

Now, update the Bayesian Network with these probabilities.

P(B)
0.2

B	P(A)
t	0.692
f	0.308

A	P(M)
t	0.308
f	0.692

This is one step of EM algorithm. The whole procedure is repeated until the probabilities stop changing.

26 How are True Positive Rate and Recall related?

True Positive Rate is same as Recall, and is also known as sensitivity. The formula to calculate them is:

$$Recall = \frac{TP}{TP + FN}, \tag{5.4}$$

where TP = true positive (both the actual and the predicted class labels are positive) and FN = false negative (the actual class label is positive whereas the predicted label is negative).

Recall (or True Positive Rate) measures the proportion of actual positive instances which are correctly predicted as positive.

27 Differentiate between ROC curve and PR curve.

A ROC curve plots the True Positive Rate (TPR) against the False Positive Rate (FPR).

$$TPR = \frac{TP}{TP + FN}, \tag{5.5}$$

$$FPR = \frac{FP}{FP + TN}, \tag{5.6}$$

where TP = true positive, TN = true negative, FP = false positive, FN = false negative. The goal is to getting no false positives.

A PR curve, on the other hand, plots Precision vs Recall.

$$Precision = \frac{TP}{TP+FP},$$ (5.7)

$$Recall = \frac{TP}{TP+FN}$$ (5.8)

The goal is to get only the true positives with no false positives and no false negatives.

A key difference between the ROC and the PR curve is that the ROC curve is made of recall and specificity, both of which are the probabilities conditioned on the true class label. Therefore, they would be same regardless of what the probability of the binary output label, Y being 1 or true is, i.e, P(Y=1). Precision is the probability conditioned on your estimate of the class label and will thus vary if you try your classifier in different populations with different baseline P(Y=1). Since the PR curve does not use TN, it can be useful when you're interested in the positive class.

28 What is a probabilistic graphical model? What is the difference between Markov Networks and Bayesian Networks?
A probabilistic graphical model is a powerful framework which represents the conditional dependency among the random variables in a graph structure. It can be used in modeling a large number of random variables having complex interactions with each other.

The two branches of the graphical representation of the distribution are Markov Networks and Bayesian Networks. Both of them differ in the set of independence that they can encode.

(a) Bayesian Networks: When the model structure is a Directed Acyclic Graph (DAG), the model represents a factorization of the joint probability of all the random variables. The Bayesian Networks capture the conditional independence between the random variables and reduce the number of parameters required to estimate the joint probability distribution.

(b) Markov Networks: They are used when the underlying network structure is an undirected graph. They follow the Markov process, i.e., given the current state, the future states would be independent of the past states. Markov Networks represent the distribution of the sequence of the nodes.

29 Define non-negative matrix factorization. Give an example of its application.
Matrix factorization means factorizing a matrix into 2 or more matrices such that the product of these matrices approximates the actual matrix. This technique can greatly simplify the complex matrix operations and can be used to find the latent features in

the given data, such as in a Recommendation system, where it could be used to find the similarities between two users.

In non- negative matrix factorization (NMF), a matrix is factorized into 2 sub-matrices such that all the 3 matrices have no negative elements. Apart from Recommendation system, NMF can be applied to text mining, to query from a set of documents.

In this technique, a document-term matrix is constructed from the input group of documents and then factorized into term-feature and feature-document matrices. It is also known as inverted indexing since it represents the frequency of terms in each document and indexes each term which maps to the set of documents in which it is present, with the corresponding frequency. All the entries in these matrices, i.e. the frequency of the terms and the index of the documents, are non-negative.

30 How is k-Nearest Neighbors (k-NN) different from k-Means algorithm?

(a) The fundamental difference between these algorithms is that k-NN is a Supervised algorithm whereas k-means is Unsupervised in nature.

(b) k-NN is a Classification (or Regression) algorithm and k-means is a Clustering algorithm.

(c) k-NN tries to classify an observation based on its "k" surrounding neighbors. It is also known as a lazy learner because it does absolutely nothing at the training stage. On the other hand, k-means algorithm partitions the training data set into different clusters such that all the data points in a cluster are closer to each other than the data points from other clusters. The algorithm tries to maintain enough separability between these clusters.

31 How do you select the important features in the given dataset?

Feature selection is a major step in the Machine Learning pipeline. What you learn from the data and how good is it depends on how efficiently the selected features represent your dataset. We will discuss more about Feature Selection in detail in the chapter on Data Preprocessing.

Some of the ways to select the important features from the dataset are:
(a) Remove the correlated features prior to selecting the relevant features because the correlated features make their significance stronger in the training while leaving or reducing the importance of other features, resulting in the model not being able to capture other features correctly.
(b) Use linear regression and select the variables based on their p-values. P-value is the level of marginal significance which represents the probability of the occurrence of a given event under the null hypothesis, which, in our case, means that the feature is not important. So, for the features with small p-values (generally $<= 0.05$), you can reject the null hypothesis and mark that feature as important.
(c) Iteratively update each feature by either Forward Selection, Backward

Elimination or Stepwise Selection technique.

(d) Use Information Gain (the amount of information gained by knowing the value of a feature) to select the top "k" important features. Obviously, the features with the higher Information Gain are more important and would be selected for the training.

32 Let's say that the number of features, m, is much greater than the number of data instances (sample observations), n. How does it affect your model selection?

In general, you would want to have more data than the number of features in it, in order to accurately learn the model. If your dataset has a high dimension (more features than the data instances), it is very easy for your model to overfit. This problem of having a high dimensionality is known as The Curse of Dimensionality.

Regression methods such as LARS, Lasso or Ridge seem to work well under these circumstances as they tend to shrink the dimension by removing irrelevant features from the dataset. You can also try using Principal Component Analysis (PCA) for Dimensionality Reduction. We will cover all of these topics in later chapters in detail.

33 What does it mean to fit a model? How do the hyperparameters relate?

Fitting a model is the process of learning the parameters of a model using the training dataset. Parameters help define the mathematical formulas behind the Machine Learning models. Hyperparameters are the "higher-level" parameters that cannot be learned from the data. They define the properties of a model, such as the model complexity or the learning rate.

For instance, let's say that you are using a linear regression model. We know that the model would be of the form:

$$y = ax + b, \tag{5.9}$$

where y represents the outcome that you want to predict and x represents the input data. a and b are the parameters that you have to optimize in order to find the best prediction for your data. Finding these parameters is known as fitting the model.

```
# In this example, we will use the same iris
# dataset and train Linear Regression model.

from sklearn.linear_model import LinearRegression
from sklearn import datasets

[X_train, y_train] = datasets.load_iris(return_X_y=True)
model = LinearRegression()
model.fit(X_train, y_train)

# After fitting, let's see what do we get as
# the coefficients and the intercept
print("Model Coefficients are " + str(model.coef_))
print("Model Intercept is " + str(model.intercept_))
```

34 What is the difference between Stochastic Gradient Descent (SGD) and standard Gradient Descent (GD)?

Both the techniques are used to find a set of parameters which minimize the loss function (the cost associated with the specific weights of the features) by evaluating them against the data. In the case of standard gradient descent, you evaluate all the training samples for each set of parameters. It is a batch update process.

In stochastic gradient descent, you evaluate the training samples one by one for the set of parameters before updating them. It is called stochastic (online) as it takes one data instance at a time, updates the parameters and uses the updated parameters for the next data instance. Stochastic gradient takes small and quick steps towards the solution.

35 When would you use standard Gradient Descent over Stochastic Gradient Descent, and vice-versa?

Standard Gradient Descent theoretically minimizes the error function better than Stochastic Gradient Descent. However, Stochastic Gradient Descent converges much faster once the dataset becomes large.

Thus standard Gradient Descent is preferable for small datasets while Stochastic Gradient Descent is preferable for the larger ones.

In practice, however, Stochastic Gradient Descent is used for most of the applications because it minimizes the error function well enough while being much faster and more memory efficient for large datasets.

36 What could be the reasons for Gradient Descent to converge slowly or not converge at all in various Machine Learning algorithms?

(a) If the step size or learning rate is too small, your function will take a long time to converge, and if it is too large, your function may jump around the optimum value and not converge.

(b) It may converge slowly in case of a Symmetric Positive Definite (SPD) matrix. The eigenvalues lay down the curvature of the function, and in case of SPD, they are all positive and generally different, which leads to a non-circular contour. Due to this, converging to the optimal point would take a lot of steps. In short, the more circular the contour is, the faster your algorithm would converge.

(c) Sometimes, due to the rounding errors, the Gradient Descent may not converge at all. The gradient descent method generally stops when the expected cost/error is either zero or very small. However, due to the rounding errors, your error might never become absolute zero, in which case your algorithm would keep converging.

(d) If your function does not have a minimum, the gradient descent would continue to descend forever.

(e) Some functions are not differentiable in certain regions, and the gradient cannot be calculated at those points.

37 How much data should you allocate for your training, validation, and test datasets?

There is no single right answer for distributing the data among training, validation and test datasets. If your training set is too small, your actual model parameters will have high variance and won't be able to learn accurately. If your test set is too small, you'll have an unreliable estimation of model performance (performance statistic will have high variance).

A good rule of thumb is to split the training and test dataset in the ratio 80:20. The training dataset can be further divided into training and validation datasets or into partitions for cross-validation, to avoid overfitting.

38 What if your dataset is skewed (e.g. 99.92% positive and 0.08% negative labels)?

Having skewed classes in a dataset is not an uncommon problem and can occur when your dataset has one class over-represented. For instance, in detecting a Fraud credit card transaction, a large percentage of the dataset would be authentic transactions made by the cardholder and a very small part would be a fraud transaction. In such a scenario, it could be very easy for your model to almost always predict "genuine" for each transaction, which is not correct.

Hence, it is essential for you to check if your dataset is suffering from skewed classes problem and take relevant measures to overcome it. Some of the ways to mitigate this issue are:

(a) Collect more data to make it even.

(b) Perform Undersampling or Oversampling of the dataset to correct for the imbalances.

(c) Use one class learning algorithm - Learn to de-noise the data instead of a traditional classification algorithm. One-class learning tries to identify the data belonging to a specific class by learning from the training set with only the observations of that class.

(d) Use asymmetric cost function (unequal weighting for different classes) to artificially balance the training process.

39 What do you mean by paired t-test? Where would you use it?

A paired t-test is a statistical procedure which is used to determine whether the mean difference between two sets of observations is zero or not. It has 2 hypotheses, the null hypothesis and the alternative hypothesis.

The null hypothesis (H_0) assumes that the true mean difference (μ_d) between the paired samples is zero.

H_0: $\mu_d = 0$

Conversely, the alternative hypothesis assumes that μ_d is not equal to zero. Depending on the expected outcome, it can take either of the 3 forms:

H_1: $\mu_d \neq 0$ (two-tailed)
H_1: $\mu_d > 0$ (upper-tailed)
H_1: $\mu_d < 0$ (lower-tailed)

We use paired t-test to compare the means of the two samples in which the observations in one sample can be paired with the observations in the other sample.

40 Define F-test. Where would you use it?

An F-test is any statistical hypothesis test where the test statistic follows an F-distribution under the null hypothesis. If you have 2 models that have been fitted to a dataset, you can use F-test to identify the model which best fits the sample population.

41 What is a chi-squared test?

A chi-squared test is any statistical hypothesis test where the test statistic follows a chi-squared distribution (a distribution of the sum of squared standard normal deviates) under the null hypothesis. It measures how well the observed distribution of data fits with the expected distribution if the variables are independent.

42 What is a p-value? Why is it important?

While performing a statistical hypothesis test, a p-value represents the level of marginal significance. It provides the smallest level of significance at which you can reject the null hypothesis. A small p-value (generally $<= 0.05$) means that there is a strong evidence against the null hypothesis, and therefore, you can reject the null hypothesis. A large p-value (> 0.05) signifies a weak evidence against the null hypothesis, and thus, you can not reject the null hypothesis. The smaller the p-value, the higher the significance with which you can reject the null hypothesis.

43 What is an F1 score?

The F1 score is a measure of a model's accuracy. It is the weighted average of the precision and recall of a model. The result ranges between 0 and 1, with 0 being the worst and 1 being the best model. F1 score is widely used in the fields of Information Retrieval and Natural Language Processing.

$$\text{F1 score} = 2 * \frac{\text{Precision} * \text{Recall}}{\text{Precision} + \text{Recall}} \qquad (5.10)$$

44 What do you understand by Type I and Type II errors?

Type I error occurs if you reject the null hypothesis when it was true, also known as False Positive. Type II error occurs if you accept the null hypothesis when it was false, also known as False Negative.

This page

intentionally

left blank

6. Supervised Learning

Supervised Learning belongs to the branch of Machine Learning which uses the labeled dataset to infer a function that maps the input to the output. It is called Supervised Learning because it contains the output labels in the training dataset.

Supervised Learning can be broadly divided into 3 categories:

1. Classification
2. Regression
3. Regularization

6.1 Classification

Classification is an approach where the output label is discrete or categorical. The objective in the classification problems is to find the corresponding output label or category to which the test instance belongs to.

Now let's dive into the most important and frequently asked interview questions from this topic.

1 **Name some of the classification algorithms that you know of.**
   Decision Trees, K-Nearest Neighbors, Naive Bayes, Support Vector Machines, and Random Forests are some of the most commonly used Classification techniques.

   We will delve into further detail on each of these topics later in this chapter.

2 What are the trade-offs between the different types of classification algorithms? How do you choose the best one?

There is no single correct answer to know the best technique. You generally begin with a heuristic approach to select a particular technique based on the problem. Most of the times, you have to test run and compare the performance of various models to see which one is more suitable for your case.

For the smaller training dataset, high bias/low variance classifiers (e.g. Naive Bayes) have an advantage over low bias/high variance classifiers (e.g. k-Nearest Neighbors), as the latter will overfit the dataset. But as the size of the training dataset grows, the latter starts performing better as they have a lower asymptotic error.

If the Naive Bayes conditional independence assumption actually holds, it will converge faster than the discriminative models such as logistic regression.

Decision Trees are easy to interpret. They easily handle feature interactions and are not affected by the outliers. One disadvantage is that they do not support online learning, so you have to rebuild the tree whenever the new data comes in. Another disadvantage is that they can easily overfit, but you can use ensembles like Random Forests to overcome that problem.

Support Vector Machines can be highly accurate and with non-linear kernels, they can model non-linearly separable dataset. They generally do not overfit. One of the disadvantages of using an SVM is that choosing the right kernel method can be tricky. Also, SVMs may incur huge memory overhead because they need to store the Support Vectors.

3 What is a Bayesian Classifier?

A Bayesian classifier is a probabilistic model which tries to minimize the probability of misclassification. From the training dataset, it calculates the probabilities of the values of the features, given the class labels and uses this information in the test dataset to predict the class given (some of) the feature values by using the Bayes rule.

4 What are the advantages of the Bayesian Network representation?

A Bayesian Network is a probabilistic graphical model which represents the features and their conditional dependencies via a Directed Acyclic Graph (DAG). Some of the advantages of representing the input data as a Bayesian Network are as follows:

(a) It captures the independence and the conditional independence where they exist.

(b) It encodes the relevant portion of the full joint among variables where dependencies exist.

(c) It uses a graphical representation which provides insight into the complexity of the inference.

(d) It is also very helpful while dealing with the missing values. Because it understands the structure of the features, this makes it easier to learn the missing parameters.

5 How can you use Naive Bayes classifier for the categorical features? What if some features are numerical?

You can use any kind of predictor in a Naive Bayes classifier. All it needs is the conditional probability of a feature given the class, i.e., P(F | Class).

For the categorical features, you can estimate P(F | Class) using a distribution such as multinomial or Bernoulli. For the numerical features, you can estimate P(F | Class) using a distribution such as Normal or Gaussian.

Since Naive Bayes assumes the conditional independence of the features, it can use different types of features together. You can calculate each feature's conditional probability and multiply them to get the final prediction.

6 Why is Naive Bayes called "naive"?

Naive Bayes assumes that all the features in a dataset are equally important and conditionally independent of each other, i.e, given a class label, Y, each feature is conditionally independent of each other. These assumptions are rarely true in the real world scenario which is why Naive Bayes is called "naive".

7 Compare Naive Bayes approach with Logistic Regression.

Following are the major differences between Naive Bayes and Logistic Regression:

(a) Naive Bayes assumes conditional independence among the features, which is not true in most of the real-life problems. When these assumptions are incorrect, Logistic Regression would be less biased because of the learned weights (parameters). Therefore, it will outperform Naive Bayes when given lots of training data.

(b) If the number of features is n, then the time complexity of Naive Bayes is O(log n), whereas that of logistic regression is O(n). So, Naive Bayes converges more quickly to its (perhaps less accurate) asymptotic estimates. Hence, it will outperform Logistic Regression in case of a small training dataset.

8 What is the difference between a generative approach and a discriminative approach? Give an example of each.

A generative model learns the joint probability distribution p(x, y) whereas a discriminative model learns the conditional probability distribution p(y | x) where y is the output class label and x is the input variable.

The former model learns the distribution of the individual classes whereas the latter learns the boundary between the classes. Naive Bayes is a generative approach as it generates the joint probability distribution of the features and the output label using P(Y) and P(X | Y), whereas Logistic Regression is a discriminative approach because it tries to find a hyperplane which separates the classes.

As you can see, generative algorithms have discriminative properties in them, since you can get P(Y | X) from P(Y) and P(X | Y) using the Bayes Theorem but the discriminative algorithms do not have generative properties.

9 Explain prior probability, likelihood and marginal likelihood in the context of Naive Bayes algorithm.

Prior probability is the proportion of dependent (binary) variable in the dataset. It is the closest guess you can make about a class, without any further information. For example, let's say that you have a dataset in which the dependent variable is binary, spam or not spam. The proportion of spam is 75% and not spam is 25%. Hence, you can estimate that there are 75% chances that any new email would be a spam.

Likelihood is the probability of classifying a given observation as true in the presence of some other variable. For example, the probability that the word "CASH" is used in the previous spam message is a likelihood.

Marginal likelihood is the probability that the word "CASH" is used in any message.

10 Define laplace estimate. What is m-estimate?

Consider a binary feature F, which can take 2 values, true and false. Now, in the training dataset, if there is no instance in which the value of F is true, then your model will conclude that the value of F can never be true, i.e., the probability of F = true is 0, which is an extreme approach.

Hence, laplace estimate serves as a fail-safe option. Instead of estimating the parameters directly, Laplace estimate uses a prior belief for each feature:

$$P(F = true) = \frac{n_{true} + 1}{\sum_{v \in Values(F)} (n_v + 1)} \qquad (6.1)$$

where n_v represents the number of instances where the value of F is v (in our case, v can be either true or false).

M-estimates is a more general approach in which:

$$P(F = x) = \frac{n_x + p_x * m}{(\sum_{v \in Values(F)} (n_v)) + m} \qquad (6.2)$$

where p_x is the prior probability of the feature F having the value x and m is the number of "virtual" instances, which represents the confidence you have in your prior estimate p_x. You can assume that F is uniformly distributed if you do not have any knowledge of p. In general, you should choose a small value of m as a higher value could distort your data more.

If you select m as the number of unique values that F could take and p_x as a

CRACKING THE MACHINE LEARNING INTERVIEW

uniformly distributed value, then $p_x * m = 1$, and m-estimate would become laplace estimate.

11 What is a confusion matrix? Explain it for a 2-class problem.

A confusion matrix is a table layout which describes the performance of a model on the test dataset for which the true values are known. For a binary or 2-class classification, which can take two values, 0 or false and 1 or true, a confusion matrix can be drawn as:

	Predicted Value 0	Predicted Value 1
Actual Value 0	True Negative (TN)	False Positive (FP)
Actual Value 1	False Negative (FN)	True Positive (TP)

From the confusion matrix, you can calculate a list of metrics to evaluate the model. Some of them are:

(a) Recall or True Positive Rate, $\frac{TP}{FN + TP}$

(b) Precision, $\frac{TP}{FP + TP}$

(c) Accuracy, $\frac{TP + TN}{TP + TN + FP + FN}$

(d) Misclassification Rate, $\frac{FP + FN}{FN + TP + TN + FP}$

```python
import matplotlib.pyplot as plt
import pandas as pd
import itertools
from sklearn import svm
from sklearn import datasets
from sklearn.model_selection import train_test_split
from sklearn.metrics import confusion_matrix, \
    classification_report

# Let's use our iris dataset.
iris = datasets.load_iris()

# For simplicity, let's just use 2 classes from our data.
# We will remove all the rows from input data
# where target class is 2

target = pd.DataFrame(iris.target)
rows_to_del = target.loc[target[0] == 2]
target = target.drop(rows_to_del.index)

data = pd.DataFrame(iris.data)
data = data.drop(rows_to_del.index)

# Now, we will split the data into train and test dataset.
X_train, X_test, y_train, y_test = train_test_split(data,
    target, test_size=0.10)
```

```
# Let's build a linear SVM classifier.
classifier = svm.SVC(kernel='linear', C=0.05)
classifier.fit(X_train, y_train)
y_pred = classifier.predict(X_test)
confusion_mtx = confusion_matrix(y_test, y_pred)

# Here, we will plot the Confusion Matrix
title = "Confusion Matrix"
fig, ax = plt.subplots()
ax.matshow(confusion_mtx, cmap=plt.cm.Blues)

threshold = confusion_mtx.max() / 2.
for i, j in itertools.product(range(confusion_mtx.shape[0]),
                              range(confusion_mtx.shape[1])):
    ax.text(i, j, format(confusion_mtx[i, j], 'd'),
            horizontalalignment="center",
            verticalalignment="center",
            color="white" if confusion_mtx[i, j] > threshold
                else "black")

plt.tight_layout()
plt.show()

# You can get all the metrics from
# classification_report of the model
print("Classification Report")
print(classification_report(y_test, y_pred))
```

12 Compare Logistic Regression with Decision Trees.

Decision Tree partitions the feature space into smaller and smaller subspaces, whereas Logistic Regression fits a single hyper-surface to divide the feature space exactly into two. When the classes are not well-separated, decision trees are susceptible to overfitting whereas Logistic Regression generalizes better.

Decision Tree is more prone to overfitting whereas Logistic Regression, being simple and having less variance, is less prone to overfitting. So, for datasets with very high dimensionality, it is better to use Logistic Regression to avoid the Curse of Dimensionality.

Decision Trees can be used where the number of dimensions is less as they can learn complex relationships among the features.

13 How can you choose a classifier based on the size of training set?

If the training set is small, the high bias/low variance models, such as Naive Bayes, tend to perform better because they are less likely to overfit. If the training set, on the other hand, is large, then, low bias/high variance models, such as Logistic Regression, tend to perform better because they can reflect more complex relationships.

14 What do you understand by the term "decision boundary"?

A decision boundary or a decision surface is a hypersurface which divides the underlying feature space into two subspaces, one for each class. If the decision boundary is a hyperplane, then the classes are linearly separable. In Figure 6.1, the

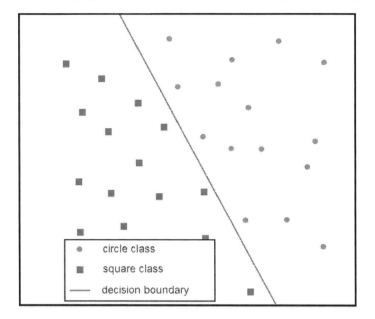

Figure 6.1: Decision Boundary

red line is the decision boundary separating the green circle instances from the blue square ones.

15 What is PAC Learning?

PAC (Probably Approximately Correct) learning is a framework used for mathematical analysis. A PAC Learner tries to learn a concept (approximately correct) by selecting a hypothesis from a set of hypotheses which has a low generalization error.

In the context of Machine Learning, a problem is PAC-learnable if there is an algorithm A when given some independently drawn samples, will produce a hypothesis with a small error for any distribution D and any concept c, and that too with a high probability.

It may not be possible to find a perfect hypothesis with zero error so the goal is to find a consistent hypothesis which can predict approximately correctly with an upper bound on the error.

Next, we will cover the most important and frequently used Classification Techniques which are Decision Trees, Ensembles, K-Nearest Neighbors, Logistic Regression, Support Vector Machines and Neural Networks. Each one of these techniques is discussed separately in the following sections. You can expect a majority of the interview questions on Classification problems from them.

6.1.1 Decision Trees

1 What is a Decision Tree?

As the name suggests, a Decision Tree uses a tree-like structure, as a predictive model, to explicitly represent the decision and decision making. Each internal node of the Decision Tree is a feature and each outgoing edge from that node represents the value that the feature can take.

In case of a categorical feature, the number of outgoing edges is the number of different values in that categories. In case of a numerical feature, the number of outgoing edges is generally two, one in which the feature value is less than a real-valued number and other in which it is greater.

Each leaf node represents a class label. The feature at each node is chosen based on the Information Gain and the one with the maximum gain is more important and is chosen at a higher level (closer to the root node).

For instance, in Figure 6.2, we have a binary output variable having values *yes* or *no* and categorical features *occupation*, *funded* and *pension*. The *occupation* is the most important feature and based on its values, the decision tree further branches out, finally predicting the output.

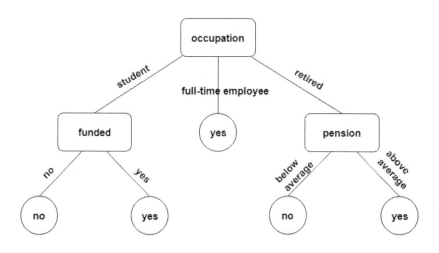

Figure 6.2: Sample Decision Tree

```
import matplotlib.pyplot as plt

# Decision Tree Classifier is part of the
# tree module in Scikit-Learn.
from sklearn.tree import DecisionTreeClassifier,\
                          plot_tree

# Let's use the standard iris dataset
# to train our model.
from sklearn import datasets
```

```
[iris_data, iris_target] = datasets.load_iris(
                               return_X_y=True)

dtree = DecisionTreeClassifier()
dtree.fit(iris_data, iris_target)

# tree module provides a plot_tree
# method to visualize the tree.
plt.figure()
plot_tree(decision_tree=dtree)
plt.show()
```

2 What are some of the reasons where you would want to use a Decision Tree model?

When you fit a Decision Tree to a training dataset, the top few nodes on which the tree is split are basically the most important features in the dataset and thus, you can use it as the feature selection technique to select the most relevant features in the dataset. Decision trees are also insensitive to outliers since the splitting happens based on the proportion of samples within the split ranges and not on the absolute values.

Because of their tree like structure, they are very easy to understand and interpret. They do not need the data to be normalized and work well even when the features have a nonlinear relationship with each other.

3 What are the some of the disadvantages of using a Decision Tree algorithm?

(a) Even a small change in input data can, at times, cause large changes in the tree as it may drastically impact the information gain used by Decision Trees to select the features.

(b) Decision trees moreover, examine only a single field at a time, leading to rectangular classification boxes. This may not correspond well with the actual distribution of records in the decision space.

(c) Decision Trees are inadequate when it comes to applying regression and predicting continuous values. A continuous variable can have an infinite number of values within an interval, capturing which, in a tree having only a finite number of branches and leaves, is very hard.

(d) There is a possibility of duplication with the same sub-tree on different paths, leading to complex trees.

(e) Every feature in the tree is forced to interact with every feature further up the tree. This is extremely inefficient if there are features that have no or weak interactions.

4 Define entropy.

Entropy is a measure of uncertainty associated with a random variable, Y. It is the expected number of bits required to communicate the value of the variable.

$$Entropy, H(Y) = - \sum_{y \in Values(Y)} (P(y) * log_2 P(y)),$$ (6.3)

where P(y) is the probability of Y having the value y. With respect to Decision Trees, the entropy is used to find the best feature split at any node.

5 What do you mean by information gain?

Information gain is used to identify the best feature to split the given training dataset. It selects the split S that most reduces the conditional entropy of output Y for the training set D.

In simple terms, the Information Gain is the change in the Entropy, H from a prior state to a new state when split on a feature:

$$InfoGain(D, S) = H_D(Y) - H_D(Y|S)$$ (6.4)

We calculate Information Gain for all the features and the feature with the highest gain is chosen as the most important feature among all the features.

6 How can the Information Gain be biased or less optimal?

Information gain is biased towards the tests with many outcomes. For instance, consider a feature that uniquely identifies each training instance. Splitting on this feature would result in many branches, each of which is "pure" (has instances of only one class) i.e, maximal information gain and this affects the model's generalization accuracy.

To address this limitation, the C4.5 algorithm uses a splitting criterion known as the Gain Ratio. Gain Ratio normalizes the Information gain by dividing it by the entropy of the split being considered, thereby avoiding the unjustified favoritism of Information Gain.

$$GainRatio(D, S) = \frac{InfoGain(D, S)}{H_D(S)} = \frac{H_D(Y) - H_D(Y|S)}{H_D(S)}$$ (6.5)

7 How do you build a Decision Tree model?

It involves determining the candidate split given a dataset, and finding the best split (either using Information Gain or Gain Ratio) from them. The current node of the tree (starting from root) is split on this feature with the maximum information gain and is divided into child nodes, with one node for each feature value.

The pseudo code for building a Decision Tree is as follows:

```
1:  procedure BUILDSUBTREE (SET OF TRAINING INSTANCES D)
2:      C ← Determine the candidate splits(D)
3:      if stopping criteria met then
4:          make a leaf node N
5:          determine the class label for N
6:      else
7:          make an internal node N
8:          S ← Find the best split(C, D)
9:          for each outcome o of S
10:             D_o ← subset of instances that have outcome o
11:             o^{th} child of N ← BuildSubTree(D_o)
            return the subtree rooted at N
```

8 Describe some of the splitting rules used by different Decision Tree algorithms.

(a) Information Gain - Already described earlier in this section.

(b) Gain Ratio - Already described earlier in this section.

(c) Permutation test - The labels of the original data are permuted and the statistic to be tested is calculated for the relabeled data for all the possible permutations of the labels. The test statistic's value for the original data is compared with the values obtained over all permutations, by calculating the percentage of the latter that is at least as extreme as the former. This percentage constitutes the significance level at which the null hypothesis can be rejected.

(d) Multi-variate split - Multivariate decision trees can use splits that contain more than one attribute at each internal node.

(e) Gini - It is a measure of how often a randomly chosen instance from the dataset would be incorrectly labeled if it was labeled randomly according to the distribution of labels in the subset.

9 Is using an ensemble like Random Forest always good?

Although using an ensemble may seem a better approach than a single Decision Tree, but ensembles have their own limitations. For instance:

(a) Ensembles generally do not perform well when the relationship between dependent and independent variables is highly linear.

(b) Unlike Decision Trees, the classification made by Random Forests is difficult to interpret easily.

(c) Another obvious shortcoming is the excessive time and computational cost of using an Ensemble over a single Decision Tree.

10 What is pruning? Why is it important?

Pruning is a technique which reduces the complexity of the final classifier by removing the sub-trees from it whose existence does not impact the accuracy of the model. In pruning, you grow the complete tree and then iteratively prune back some nodes until further pruning is harmful. This is done by evaluating the impact of pruning each node on the tuning (validation) dataset accuracy and greedily removing the one that most improves the tuning dataset accuracy.

One simple way of pruning a Decision Tree is to impose a minimum on the number of training examples that reach a leaf. Pruning keeps the trees simple without affecting the overall accuracy. It helps solve the overfitting issue by reducing the size as well as the complexity of the tree.

```python
from sklearn.tree import DecisionTreeClassifier
from sklearn import datasets
from sklearn.model_selection import train_test_split
from sklearn.metrics import classification_report

iris = datasets.load_iris()
X_train, X_test, y_train, y_test = train_test_split(iris.data
    , iris.target, test_size=0.40)

# DecisionTreeClassifier offers various parameters to
# prune your tree, such as:
#    max_depth: Limit the depth of the tree to
#               make it a generalized model.
#    max_leaf_nodes: Limit the number of leaf nodes.
#    min_samples_leaf: Minimum samples in a leaf node.

# Let's use different options and see how our accuracy varies

# Model 1
model = DecisionTreeClassifier(max_depth=2, max_leaf_nodes=5,
    min_samples_leaf=10)
model.fit(X_train, y_train)
y_pred = model.predict(X_test)
print(classification_report(y_test, y_pred))

# Model 2
model = DecisionTreeClassifier(max_depth=10, max_leaf_nodes
    =10, min_samples_leaf=30)
model.fit(X_train, y_train)
y_pred = model.predict(X_test)
print(classification_report(y_test, y_pred))
```

6.1.2 Ensembles

1 What is Ensemble Learning?

Ensemble Learning is a process in which multiple individual Machine Learning models, such as classifiers, are strategically generated and combined to solve a particular computational program.

In contrast to the standard Machine Learning approach, Ensemble Learning constructs and combines a set of hypotheses for prediction. Ensemble Learning boosts the weak learners (learners which perform very poorly and are only slightly better than a random guess) and improves the overall prediction accuracy.

2 What is an Ensemble?

An ensemble is a set of learned models whose individual decisions are combined in some way to make better predictions for the test instances. Predictions using ensembles typically require more computation as compared to a single model so you can think of ensembles as a way to trade-off the weak learners by performing extra computation.

Some of the common ensemble techniques include Bagging, Boosting, Bayes Optimal Classifier and Stacking.

3 Why do you need Ensemble Learning?

Ensemble Learning is used to improve the classification, prediction, function approximation etc of a model, by combining multiple individual learned models.

It reduces the variance by averaging out the outputs from the individual models. Another benefit of using an ensemble is that it helps overcome the overfitting problem, which could occur in a single model.

4 When should you use Ensemble Learning?

Ensemble Learning is used when you build component classifiers that are more accurate and independent of each other. They can be used in cases where the training dataset is noisy and/or contains outliers. They are generally slow, so if speed is not a big concern, you can use ensembles over Decision Trees.

5 Differentiate between Bagging and Boosting.

Bootstrap aggregating, also called Bagging, is a Machine Learning Ensemble algorithm designed to improve the stability and accuracy of the Machine Learning algorithms used in statistical classification and regression. It reduces the variance and helps to avoid overfitting.

Boosting is a Machine Learning Ensemble algorithm used primarily for reducing the bias. It belongs to a family of Machine Learning algorithms which convert the weak learners to the strong ones.

Bagging is an equally weighted average whereas Boosting gives more weight to those with better performance on the training dataset. Since Bagging uses random sampling of the data to train each model, it can execute the training stage in parallel. Whereas Boosting builds each model sequentially by weighing the data based on previous model's accuracy, and thus cannot run in parallel for the training purpose.

Bagging works mainly by reducing the variance and Boosting works by primarily reducing the bias.

If the individual model is suffering from very low performance, it is better to use Boosting as it reduced the bias. But if the issue is overfitting, then Bagging is a better option than Boosting as Bagging reduces overfitting.

6 Tell me about Random Forests. What are the major differences between Random Forests and Support Vector Machines (SVMs)?
Random Forest is an Ensemble Learning method which operates by constructing a multitude of Decision Trees at the training time and outputting the class label that is the mode (most commonly occurring value) of the classes (for classification) or the mean prediction (for regression) of the individual trees.

Some of the major differences between Random Forests and Support Vector Machines are:

(a) Random Forests are intrinsically suited for multi-class problems, while SVMs are intrinsically two-class. In case of SVMs, you would need to reduce a multi-class problem into multiple binary classification problems.

(b) Random Forests work well with a mixture of numerical and categorical features. Whereas, SVMs maximize the margin between the two classes and thus rely on the concept of "distance" between the different points.

(c) SVM models perform better on sparse data (dataset in which most of the values are zeros) than the trees in general. A major reason behind it is the kernel methods used by SVMs which do not depend on the input dimension of the feature space.

(d) Random Forests can be trained in parallel, something that cannot be done with SVM. This is because a Random Forest consists of multiple Decision Trees which can be learned simultaneously and independent of each other.

(e) Random Forests are fairly robust and have very little need for tuning of hyper-parameters. (A hyper-parameter is a parameter whose value is set before the learning process begins, such as learning rate, epochs etc. On the contrary, the values of the other parameters are learned via training.)

7 On what type of Ensemble technique is a Random Forest based? What particular limitation does it try to address?

Random Forest is an Ensemble method in which a classifier is constructed by combining several different independent base classifiers. It is based on the bagging algorithm and is designed to improve the model's accuracy. It also helps in reducing the variance and overfitting.

8 Both being tree based algorithms, how is Random Forest different from Gradient Boosting algorithm (GBM)?

The fundamental difference between Random Forest and GBM is that the Random Forest uses bagging technique to make predictions and GBM uses boosting technique to make predictions. Random Forest improves the model's accuracy by reducing the variance (mainly). The trees grown are uncorrelated so as to maximize the decrease in variance. On the other hand, GBM improves the accuracy by primarily reducing the bias in the model.

6.1.3 K-Nearest Neighbors

As the name suggests, k-Nearest Neighbors (k-NN) is a technique which predicts the output label of the test example based on the labels of the closest k nearest neighbors from the training dataset.

1 **Walk me through the k-Nearest Neighbors algorithm.**

k-NN is a lazy learner algorithm, i.e., it does not do anything at the time of training. Below are the steps performed at the time of testing. For any new test example, k-NN

(a) first computes its distance from all the examples in the training dataset,

(b) then selects the k training examples with the lowest distances,

(c) and finally predicts the output label of the test example by either choosing the most occurring label from the selected training examples (in case of Classification) or by calculating the mean of them (in case of Regression).

Let's take an example of a k-NN Classification problem. Suppose you have the following training dataset:

	Height (in cm)	Weight (in kg)	Type
Instance 1	150	45	Normal
Instance 2	160	80	Obese
Instance 3	165	75	Overweight
Instance 4	170	70	Normal
Instance 5	175	75	Normal

Now, let's say that you want to find the type for a person whose height is 180 cm, weight is 75 kgs and you have chosen k=3.

First you need to calculate his distance from all the training instances:

Distance(test person, instance 1) = $\sqrt{(180 - 150)^2 + (75 - 45)^2} = 42.4$
Distance(test person, instance 2) = $\sqrt{(180 - 160)^2 + (75 - 80)^2} = 20.6$
Distance(test person, instance 3) = $\sqrt{(180 - 165)^2 + (75 - 75)^2} = 15$
Distance(test person, instance 4) = $\sqrt{(180 - 170)^2 + (75 - 70)^2} = 11.2$
Distance(test person, instance 5) = $\sqrt{(180 - 175)^2 + (75 - 75)^2} = 5$

Based on the distances, you can see that the instance 5, 4 and 3 are the 3 closest neighbors of the test person. Taking the most ocurring label from these instances, you would label the test person as "Normal".

```
# K Nearest Neighbors classifier is present as
# KNeighborsClassifier class in neighbors module.
from sklearn.neighbors import KNeighborsClassifier

# Let's create input dataset discussed in our solution
X = [[150, 45],
     [160, 80],
     [165, 75],
     [170, 70],
     [175, 75]]
Y = ["Normal", "Obese", "Overweight", "Normal", "Normal"]
k = 3

# Let's create the K nearest neighbors classifier
# with 3 neighbors
classifier = KNeighborsClassifier(n_neighbors=k)

# Now, train our classifier on the input dataset
classifier.fit(X, Y)

# Let's see what it predicts for the person whose
# height is 180cm and weight is 75kgs.
print(classifier.predict([[180, 75]]))

# As you can see, it also predicts the person type as 'Normal
# '.
```

2 **What are some of the advantages and disadvantages of using k-Nearest Neighbors method?**

Advantages:

(a) They are simple to implement, lazy learners which means that no training is required. They are run at the time of testing.

(b) They are very flexible to feature/distance choices.

(c) They can naturally handle multi-class models.

(d) Given enough representative training dataset, they can achieve sufficiently good accuracy.

Disadvantages:

(a) Since they require all the training dataset while testing, storage can be an issue for large dataset.

(b) They need a large number of sample data to find the nearest neighbors.

(c) Often, the distance function needs a decent meaning as you need to calculate the distance between the features.

(d) Prediction time can be costly when the training dataset is large.

3 Can you use k-NN in regression?

Yes, k-Nearest Neighbor can be used for regression problems as well. In this case, the response value of the test instance can be either the mean or the median of the output values of the k nearest neighbors.

4 How do you choose the optimal k in k-NN?

There is no hard and fast rule to select the optimal value of "k". It varies from dataset to dataset. In general, you would want to keep it small enough to exclude the samples of the other classes but large enough to minimize any noise in the data. One way to choose the optimal k is to try different values of k from 1 to 10 and use Cross-Validation to select the value which results in the best accuracy.

5 Can you tell me some of the common distance metrics used in k-NN?

Let x and y be two data instances (examples) whose distance you want to compute. Let us say you have N features. So, x_1 is the value of feature 1 in x, y_1 is the value of feature 1 in y, x_2 is the value of feature 2 in x and so on.

Following are a few metrics that can be used to calculate the distance between the two feature values:

(a) Euclidean Distance - Used for continuous features and is given by the formula:

$$d(x,y) = \sqrt{\sum_{i=1}^{N}(x_i - y_i)^2} \tag{6.6}$$

(b) Manhattan Distance - Used for continuous features and is given by the formula:

$$d(x,y) = \sum_{i=1}^{N}|x_i - y_i| \tag{6.7}$$

(c) Hamming Distance - Used for categorical features and is given by the number of features whose values differ from each other for x and y.

An important point here is that you can implement your own distance metric which is suitable for your problem. The above mentioned metrics are just some of the most commonly used metrics.

6 How does the value of k vary with bias and variance?

A large value of k means a simpler model as it would take the average of a large number of training examples. So, the variance (or the standard deviation) would decrease by increasing the value of k. A simpler model means underfitting and results in high bias. On the contrary, a small value of k means that the test example depends only on a small number of training examples and hence, it would result in high variance and low bias.

7 How would you vary k if there is noise in the dataset?

You should increase k to handle any noise. A large k value would average out or nullify any noise or outlier in the given dataset.

8 How can you speed up the model's classification/prediction time?

There are 2 ways to improve your k-NN's computation (including both training and testing) time:

(a) Edited nearest neighbors - Instead of retaining all the training instances, select a subset of them which can still provide accurate classifications. Use either **forward selection** or **backward elimination** to select the subset of the instances which can still represent other instances.

(b) K-dimensional Tree - It is a smart data structure used to perform nearest neighbor and range searches. A k-d tree is similar to a decision tree except that each internal node stores one data instance (i.e. each node is a k-dimensional data point) and splits on the median value of the feature having the highest variance.

6.1.4 Logistic Regression

1 Define Logistic Regression.

Logistic regression is a statistical method for analyzing a dataset in which one or more independent variables determine the outcome, that can have only a limited number of values, i.e the response variable is categorical in nature. Logistic Regression is generally the go-to method for classification problems when the response (output) variable is binary.

2 How do you train a Logistic Regression model?

You use a logistic function for training a Logistic Regression model. Given the input data x, weight vector w (coefficients of the independent variable x) and the probability of the output label y, P(y), the logistic function is calculated as:

$$P(y) = \frac{1}{1 + e^{-wx}} \tag{6.8}$$

If P(y) > 0.5, you predict the output as 1, otherwise 0. Then, based on the prediction error in the training instances, the whole process is repeated by updating the weights in each iteration. The process is stopped once you reach a good enough accuracy or complete all the iterations and the final weights are used as the values to predict the outcome of the test instances.

3 How do you estimate the coefficients in Logistic Regression?

You can estimate the values of the coefficients (weights of the independent variables) using Stochastic Gradient Descent.

For each training instance, calculate a prediction using the current values of the coefficients and based on the prediction error, update the coefficient values. Repeat this process until the accuracy reaches a threshold or the number of iterations gets exhausted.

4 How would you evaluate a Logistic Regression model?

You can use the following methods to evaluate the performance of the learned Logistic Regression model:

(a) **AUROC**: Since Logistic Regression is used to predict the probabilities, you can use AUROC (Area Under the Receiver Operating Characteristic) curve along with the confusion matrix to determine its performance.

(b) **AIC (Akaike Information Criterion)**: Also, the analogous metric of adjusted R^2 in logistic regression is AIC. AIC is the measure of fit which penalizes a model for the number of model coefficients. Therefore, we always prefer a model with the minimum AIC value.

(c) **Deviance**: We prefer the model with lower deviance value. Deviance represents the goodness of fit for a model. Null deviance means the response only has an intercept and the residual deviance indicates the response has non-zero weight vector.

5 What is a link function in Logistic Regression?

A link function provides the relationship between the expected value of the response variable and the linear predictors. The Logistic Regression uses Logit as its link function, which is nothing but the term *wx* in the equation 6.8.

6 What is the range of the Logistic Regression function?

We know that the logistic function is calculated as:

$$f = \frac{1}{1 + e^{-wx}} \qquad (6.9)$$

So, for any input wx in the range $(-\infty, \infty)$, the output of the Logistic function would lie in the range $(0,1)$.

7 When is Logistic Regression multinomial?

Logistic Regression is multinomial when the number of classes to separate are more than two. A Multinomial Logistic Regression algorithm predicts the probabilities of each possible class as the outcome.

For instance, predicting which major is a better option for the student given their grades, subjects they like and dislike, etc. is an example of a multinomial logistic regression problem.

8 Tell me about One vs All Logistic Regression.

In One Vs All, if there are *n* classes, then you have *n* different independent classification problems, one for each class. For i^{th} classification problem, you learn all the points which belong to the class *i* and all the other points are assumed to belong to a pseudo class *not i*.

For a new test data, you use the most occurring response from all the *n* classifiers to predict its output.

```
from sklearn.linear_model import LogisticRegression
from sklearn import datasets

[X, y] = datasets.load_iris(return_X_y=True)

# Create one-vs-rest logistic regression model and train it
clf = LogisticRegression(random_state=0, multi_class='ovr')
clf.fit(X, y)

# Create new observation
new_observation = [[.2, .4, .6, .8]]

# Let's predict its class
print(clf.predict(new_observation))

# The probability of the class predicted should be
# the highest among all the probabilities.
print(clf.predict_proba(new_observation))
```

9 Which metric is generally used to evaluate the performance of a Logistic Regression model?

AIC is the most widely used metric for evaluating the Logistic Regression Model's performance. (It has already been explained earlier in this section in question 4.)

10 What would you do to speed up your algorithm without compromising a lot on the model's accuracy, if your training dataset is huge?

Reducing the number of iterations would reduce the training time but it will hamper the accuracy as well. So, you should increase the learning rate to speed up the convergence while still maintaining a similar accuracy.

6.1.5 Support Vector Machines

1 What do you understand by maximal margin classifier? Why is it beneficial?

A margin classifier gives the distance of a data instance from the decision boundary. A decision boundary is a hyperplane separating the two class labels. Maximal margin classifier is a classifier which draws the separation hyperplane between the two class labels in a way such that the distance of the hyperplane from them is maximum, i.e, the hyperplane is at an equal distance from them. The maximal margin is the optimal hyperplane separating the classes and does not suffer from overfitting.

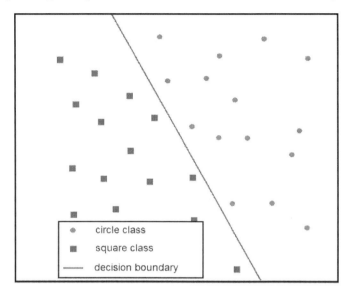

Figure 6.3: Margin classifier

```
import numpy as np
import matplotlib.pyplot as plt
from sklearn import datasets, svm

# Let's use the standard iris dataset. For simplicity,
# we will use the 1st two features only.
iris = datasets.load_iris()
X = iris.data[:, :2]
y = iris.target

# Now, let's create a linear SVM classifier instance
# and fit the iris dataset.
svc_classifier = svm.SVC(kernel='linear').fit(X, y)

# create a mesh to plot in
h = .05  # step size in the mesh
x_min, x_max = X[:, 0].min() - 1, X[:, 0].max() + 1
y_min, y_max = X[:, 1].min() - 1, X[:, 1].max() + 1
xx, yy = np.meshgrid(np.arange(x_min, x_max, h),
                     np.arange(y_min, y_max, h))

plt.subplot(2, 2, 1)
plt.subplots_adjust(wspace=0.4, hspace=0.4)
```

```
predicted_y = svc_classifier.predict(
                    np.c_[xx.ravel(), yy.ravel()])
predicted_y = predicted_y.reshape(xx.shape)
plt.contourf(xx, yy, predicted_y, cmap=plt.cm.coolwarm,
             alpha=0.6)

# Plot the input training data points
plt.scatter(X[:, 0], X[:, 1], c=y, cmap=plt.cm.coolwarm)
plt.xlabel('Sepal length')
plt.ylabel('Sepal width')
plt.xlim(xx.min(), xx.max())
plt.ylim(yy.min(), yy.max())
plt.show()
```

2 How do you train a Support Vector Machine (SVM)? What about hard SVM and soft SVM?

The goal of SVM training is to learn a hyerplane "h", which maximizes the margin between the different class labels. Suppose you have a training dataset D. Let x_+ denote the closest instance to the hyperplane among positive instances, and x_- the negative instances. Let w be the weight vector and b be the bias term. Since $w^T x + b = 0$ and $c(w^T x + b) = 0$ define the same hyperplane, you have the freedom to choose the normalization of w. Choose a normalization such that $w^T x_+ + b = 1$ and $w^T x_- + b = -1$. Then the margin is given by:

$$
\begin{aligned}
margin_D(h) &= \frac{w}{||w||_2} \cdot (x_+ - x_-) \\
&= \frac{w^T(x_+ - x_-)}{||w||_2} \\
&= \frac{2}{||w||_2}
\end{aligned}
\tag{6.10}
$$

For hard margin, train the SVM as:

$$
\min_{w,b} \frac{1}{2} ||w||_2^2
\tag{6.11}
$$

$$
s.t. y^i(w^T x^i + b) >= 1, \text{ for each training instance } i
\tag{6.12}
$$

This equation is valid only when the training instances are linearly separable. If they are not, then you cannot use hard margin SVM. In that case, you have to use soft margin SVM where you add a slack variable for penalizing each instance which falls on the other side of the margin. The corresponding equation for soft margin SVM is:

$$
\min_{w,b,\varepsilon_i} \frac{1}{2} ||w||_2^2 + C \sum_i \varepsilon_i
\tag{6.13}
$$

$$
s.t. y^i(w^T x^i + b) >= 1 - \varepsilon_i, \text{ for each training instance } i
\tag{6.14}
$$

Here, ε_i is the slack variable for i^{th} instance and C is the regularization term. Together, $C\varepsilon_i$ is the penalty incurred when x_i falls on the other side of the margin.

3 What is a kernel? Explain the Kernel trick.

Kernels can be designed and used to represent the complex data types such as strings, trees, graphs etc. A kernel is a mapping function which maps the 2 input vector spaces into a (higher dimension) space. For a dataset, there exists a mapping ϕ to a higher-dimensional space such that the data is separable in that space. Explicitly calculating that mapping is not scalable so we use kernel trick, which calculates the dot product without explicitly mapping them to a higher dimension.

Let's take an example. Consider 2-D points x and y. Now, let us assume that they are not separable in 2-D space but you can separate them after transforming to the following higher dimension:

$$\phi(x) - > x_1^2, x_2^2, \sqrt{2}x_1x_2 \tag{6.15}$$

Here ϕ is the transformation which maps x from 2-D to 3-D space. We have added $\sqrt{2}$ only for our convenience, which you would understand in a bit. Now, in order to calculate the similarity between x and y, you would need to calculate:

$$\begin{aligned} \phi(x), \phi(y) &= \{x_1^2, x_2^2, \sqrt{2}x_1x_2,\}\{y_1^2, y_2^2, \sqrt{2}y_1y_2\} \\ &= x_1^2y_1^2 + x_2^2y_2^2 + 2x_1x_2y_1y_2 \end{aligned} \tag{6.16}$$

Performing these calculations could be time consuming and their complexity could easily escalate with the high dimensional data. Instead, you can use the kernel trick which calculates the dot product of x and y:

$$\begin{aligned} K(x,y) &= (x.y)^2 \\ &= (\{x_1, x_2\}.\{y_1, y_2\})^2 \\ &= (x_1y_1 + x_2y_2)^2 \\ &= x_1^2y_1^2 + x_2^2y_2^2 + 2x_1x_2y_1y_2, \end{aligned} \tag{6.17}$$

which is same as what you get in equation 6.16 but you do not have to perform such lengthy computations. Hence, using a kernel trick greatly simplifies the calculations to separate the input vectors by using just the dot products.

4 Name some common kernels. How do you select a particular kernel for your problem?

Some of the common kernels are:

(a) Polynomial of degree d, $k(x,z) = (x.z)^d$, where x and z are the two support vectors.

(b) Polynomial of degree up to d, $k(x,z) = (x.z+1)^d$.

(c) Radial basis function (RBF) (a.k.a. Gaussian), $k(x,z) = exp(-\gamma||x-z||^2)$, where γ is the inverse of the standard deviation of the Gaussian function. A small γ means high variance implying that the two support vectors are similar to each other and vice-versa for a large value of γ.

You can start off by using a linear kernel as it is a simple one. But, if the dataset is not linearly separable, then you can use RBF kernel, as it makes a good default kernel. The choice of the kernel can be automated by optimizing a cross-validation based model selection. And, based on the loss function (or a performance metric), you can choose which kernel is appropriate for your problem.

```python
# Let's go back to the code in question 1
# and try different kernel methods.

import numpy as np
import matplotlib.pyplot as plt
from sklearn import datasets, svm

# Let's use the standard iris dataset. For simplicity,
# we will use the 1st two features only.
iris = datasets.load_iris()
X = iris.data[:, :2]
y = iris.target

# Now, let's create SVM classifier instances
# and fit the iris dataset.
linear_classifier = svm.SVC(kernel='linear')
linear_classifier.fit(X, y)

poly_classifier = svm.SVC(kernel='poly', degree=3)
poly_classifier.fit(X, y)

rbf_classifier = svm.SVC(kernel='rbf', gamma=0.8)
rbf_classifier.fit(X, y)

# create a mesh to plot in
h = .05  # step size in the mesh
x_min, x_max = X[:, 0].min() - 1, X[:, 0].max() + 1
y_min, y_max = X[:, 1].min() - 1, X[:, 1].max() + 1
xx, yy = np.meshgrid(np.arange(x_min, x_max, h),
                     np.arange(y_min, y_max, h))

titles = ['Linear SVM Classifier', 'Polynomial SVM Classifier
    ', 'RBF SVM Classifier']

for index, classifier in enumerate((linear_classifier,
                        poly_classifier, rbf_classifier)
                        ):
    plt.subplot(2, 2, index + 1)
    plt.subplots_adjust(wspace=0.4, hspace=0.4)
    predicted_y = classifier.predict(
                    np.c_[xx.ravel(), yy.ravel()])
    predicted_y = predicted_y.reshape(xx.shape)
    plt.contourf(xx, yy, predicted_y,
            cmap=plt.cm.coolwarm, alpha=0.6)
    plt.scatter(X[:, 0], X[:, 1], c=y,
            cmap=plt.cm.coolwarm)
    plt.xlabel('Sepal length')
    plt.ylabel('Sepal width')
    plt.xlim(xx.min(), xx.max())
```

```
    plt.ylim(yy.min(), yy.max())
    plt.title(titles[index])

plt.show()
```

5 When training a Support Vector Machine, what value are you optimizing for?

The SVM problem can have many possible hyperplanes which separate the positive and the negative instances. But the goal is to choose the hyperplane which maximizes the margin between the classes. The reason behind this optimization is that such a hyperplane, which not only separates the training instances but is also as far away from them as possible, would generalize the best and not result in overfitting.

6 How does a kernel method scale with the number of instances (e.g. a Gaussian rbf kernel)?

Kernel method generally constructs the kernel matrix of the order $R^{N \times N}$, where N is the number of the data instances. Hence, the complexity of a kernel function depends on the number of data instances and not on the number of features.

A kernel method scales quadratically (referring to the construction of the gram matrix), and cubic (referring to the matrix inversion) with the number of data instances.

7 Describe some of the ways to overcome the scaling issues.

Some of the ways to overcome the scaling issues in SVMs are:

(a) Nystrom Method - Kernel matrix computation varies quadratically with N, the number of data instances, which becomes a bottleneck when N becomes very large. To alleviate this issue, Nystrom approximation is used which generates a low-rank kernel matrix approximation, d « N.

(b) Taking random features, by query/nearest neighbors. This involves mapping the input data to a randomized low-dimensional feature space such that the inner products of the transformed data are approximately equal to those in the original one.

(c) Distributed/Parallel training algorithms and applying multiple SVM classifiers together.

8 What are some of the pros and cons of using Gaussian processes or general kernel methods approach to learning?

Pros:

General kernel methods can work well with non-linearly separable data, are non-parametric and more accurate in general.

Cons:

They do not scale well with the number of data instances and require hyper-parameter tuning.

9 Can you find the solutions in SVMs which are globally optimal?

Yes, since the learning task is framed as a convex optimization problem, which is bound to have one optimum solution only, and that is the global minima. There is only a single global minimum in case of SVM as opposed to the multi-layer neural network, which has multiple local minima and the solution achieved may or may not be a global minimum, depending upon the initial weights.

6.1.6 Artificial Neural Networks

1 What is an Artificial Neural Network?

An Artificial Neural Network (ANN) is a computational model inspired by the biological neural networks. ANNs can be extremely useful in cases where the traditional rule-based Machine learning models fail since ANNs try to learn automatically from the given dataset without any task specific programming.

They are used as a random function approximation tool. ANNs take data samples rather than the entire data sets, which saves the computation time. Typically, ANNs are organized in layers. The first layer consists of input neurons. They send input data on to the hidden layers (where each neuron is called a hidden unit), which in turn send the output neurons to the final output layer.

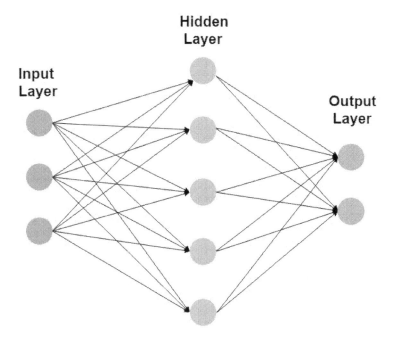

Figure 6.4: Structure of Artificial Neural Network

```
# Scikit-Learn has neural_network module which
# provides Multi-Layer Perceptron Classifier and
# Multi-Layer Perceptron Regressor classes.
from sklearn.neural_network import MLPClassifier
from sklearn import datasets
from sklearn.model_selection import train_test_split
from sklearn.metrics import classification_report

iris = datasets.load_iris()
X_train, X_test, y_train, y_test = train_test_split(iris.data
    , iris.target, test_size=0.10)

# Below code would create a Multi-Layer Perceptron
```

```
# classifier with single hidden layer having 6 hidden units.
mlp_classifier = MLPClassifier(hidden_layer_sizes=6)
mlp_classifier.fit(X_train, y_train)
y_pred = mlp_classifier.predict(X_test)
# Let's look at the metrics of this model
print(classification_report(y_test, y_pred))

# You can create multiple hidden layers as:
mlp_classifier_multi_hidden_layers = MLPClassifier(
                              hidden_layer_sizes=(6, 4, 8))
mlp_classifier_multi_hidden_layers.fit(X_train, y_train)
y_pred = mlp_classifier_multi_hidden_layers.predict(X_test)

# Let's see how the metrics change with change
# in the number of hidden layers.
print(classification_report(y_test, y_pred))

# MLPClassifier also offers parameters such as 'activation',
# 'batch_size', 'learning_rate', 'learning_rate_init' etc.
# Try and play with it by setting different values of these
# parameters and check how it affects various metrics.
```

2 What are some of the advantages and disadvantages of using an ANN?

Some of the advantages of ANN are:

(a) It is a nonlinear model that is easy to use and understand as compared to statistical methods.

(b) It has the ability to implicitly detect complex nonlinear relationships between the dependent (output) and independent (input) variables.

(c) It can easily train a large amount of data.

(d) It can be easily run in a parallel architecture, thereby drastically reducing the computational time.

(e) It is a non-parametric model (does not assume the data distribution to be based on any finite set of parameters such as mean or variance) which does not need a lot of statistics background.

However, ANN has some disadvantages too:

(a) Because of its black-box nature, it is difficult to interpret how the output is generated from the input.

(b) It can not extrapolate the results. One reason for such shortcoming can be its non-parametric nature.

(c) It can suffer from overfitting easily. Due to a large number of hidden units (neurons), ANN can create a very complex model which often leads to overfitting on the training dataset and poor performance on the test dataset. Methods such as regularization and early stopping can help generalize the model and reduce overfitting.

(d) ANN generally converges slowly.

3 What do you mean by a perceptron?

A perceptron is an algorithm which learns a binary classifier by directly mapping the input vector "x" to the output response "y" with no hidden layers.

$$y = 1 \text{ if w.x + b} > 0$$
$$0 \text{ otherwise,}$$

(6.18)

where w is a vector of real-valued weights representing the slope and b is the bias, representing the horizontal shift of the output vs input curve from the origin.

4 What is the role of the hidden units in ANNs?

Hidden units transform the input space into a new space where the perceptrons suffice. They numerically represent new features constructed from the original features in the input layer. Each hidden layer (consisting of hidden units) transforms its input layer into a new feature space which is easier for its output layer to interpret.

For instance, you may have a raw image supplied as the input layer, and the first hidden layer transforming the raw pixel data into the edges in the image, second hidden layer detecting shapes from the edges, and the output layer performing object recognition on those shapes.

5 What is an activation function?

An activation function, also known as the transfer function, is simply the output value of a hidden or output unit. It can be Identity, Sigmoid function etc.

If the input to the activation function is given by x, and its corresponding weight as w, then the:

(a) Output of Identity activation function, $f(x) = wx$.
(b) Output of Sigmoid activation function, $f(x) = \frac{1}{1+e^{-wx}}$.

```
from sklearn.neural_network import MLPClassifier
from sklearn import datasets
from sklearn.model_selection import train_test_split
from sklearn.metrics import classification_report

iris = datasets.load_iris()
X_train, X_test, y_train, y_test = train_test_split(iris.data
    , iris.target, test_size=0.10)

# MLPClassifier offers a parameter 'activation' which
# can take different values such as 'identity', 'logistic',
# 'tanh', 'relu'. Default value is 'relu'.

# You can set it as follows:
mlp_classifier = MLPClassifier(hidden_layer_sizes=6,
                                activation='identity')
mlp_classifier.fit(X_train, y_train)
```

```
y_pred = mlp_classifier.predict(X_test)

# Let's look at the metrics of this model
print(classification_report(y_test, y_pred))

mlp_classifier = MLPClassifier(hidden_layer_sizes=6,
                                 activation='tanh')
mlp_classifier.fit(X_train, y_train)
y_pred = mlp_classifier.predict(X_test)

# Let's see how the metrics change with
# change in the activation type.
print(classification_report(y_test, y_pred))
```

6 Does gradient descent converge to a global minimum in a single-layered network? In a multi-layered network?

Since a single-layered neural network is a convex function, the gradient descent is bound to converge to a global minimum. On the contrary, a multi-layered neural network is not a convex function and hence, the gradient descent may or may not converge to a global minimum, depending upon the initial weights.

7 How should you initialize the weights for sigmoid units?

The weights should be initialized with small values so that the activations are in the range where the derivative is large (learning is quicker), and random values to ensure symmetry breaking (i.e. if all weights are the same, the hidden units will all represent the same thing). Typical initial weights are in the range of [-0.01, 0.01].

8 How should you set the value of the learning rate?

The learning rate has to be initialized by hit and trial method, depending upon the particular problem. If it is set too small, the error would go down slowly and if it is set too large, the error would go up on the other side.

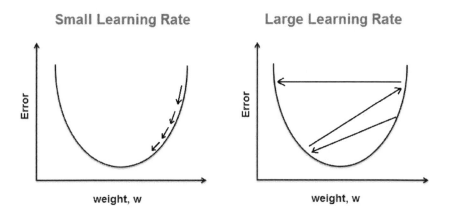

Figure 6.5: Variation in Error with Learning Rate

```
from sklearn.neural_network import MLPClassifier
from sklearn import datasets
import time

iris = datasets.load_iris()

# Let's measure the time taken for our model to
# converge with a small learning rate.
start_time = time.time()
mlp_classifier = MLPClassifier(hidden_layer_sizes=(6,4),
                               learning_rate_init=0.001)
mlp_classifier.fit(iris.data, iris.target)
end_time = time.time()
print("Time taken to converge is " +
        str(end_time - start_time) + " seconds")

# large learning rate
start_time = time.time()
mlp_classifier = MLPClassifier(hidden_layer_sizes=(6, 4),
                               learning_rate_init=0.1)
mlp_classifier.fit(iris.data, iris.target)
end_time = time.time()
print("Time taken to converge is " +
        str(end_time - start_time) + " seconds")
```

9 What is backpropagation?

Backpropagation is a method used in Artificial Neural Networks to calculate the error contribution of each neuron after a batch of data is processed. It calculates the gradient of the loss function, i.e. the rate with which the loss (cost) changes with the change in the weights and the bias. This is used to update the weights in each iteration with the goal to minimize the cost as much as possible.

10 Can backpropagation work well with multiple hidden layers?

With linear activation function, you can stack as many hidden layers as possible and the output would still be a linear combination of the input data. But with sigmoid activation function, the backpropagation does not usually work well if you have a lot of hidden layers as the diffusion of gradients leads to slow training in the lower layers.

11 What is the loss function in an Artificial Neural Network?

A loss function is a function which maps the values of one or more variables onto a real number that represents the "cost" associated with those values. For backpropagation, the loss function calculates the difference between the actual output value and its expected output. The loss function is also sometimes referred as the cost function or error function.

12 How does an Artificial Neural Network with three layers (one input layer, one hidden layer, and one output layer) compare to a Logistic Regression?

Logistic Regression, in general, can be thought of as a single layer Artificial Neural Network. It is mostly used in the cases where the classes are more or less linearly separable whereas an Artificial Neural Network can solve much more complex problems.

One of the nice properties of the Logistic Regression is that the Logistic cost function is convex, which means that you are guaranteed to find the global minimum. But, in case of a multi-layer neural network, you lose this convexity and may end up at a local minimum, depending upon the initial weights.

13 What do you understand by Rectified Linear Units?
Rectified linear unit (ReLU) is an activation function, given by $f(x) = \max(0, x)$ i.e, output is 0 for any negative input and is linear with slope 1 for all the positive input values. Because of its linear form, it greatly speeds up the convergence of stochastic gradient descent. It makes the activation sparse and efficient as it yields 0 activation for negative inputs.

But ReLU can be fragile during training, that is, the ReLU units can irreversibly die during training since they can get knocked off the data manifold. With large learning rate, a large gradient can "kill" a ReLU such that the input becomes negative. This leads to ReLU being in $f(x) = 0$ region, making the gradient 0 leading to no changes in the weights. This means that the neurons which go into this state will stop responding to any change in the error and hence die.

14 Can you explain the Tangent Activation function? How is it better than the sigmoid function?
Tangent activation function, also known as tanh function, is a hyperbolic activation function often used in Neural Networks. Its formula is:

$$g_{tanh}(x) = \frac{\sinh(x)}{\cosh(x)}$$
$$= \frac{e^x - e^{-x}}{e^x + e^{-x}}$$

(6.19)

The output of the tanh function lies in the range (-1, 1). Tanh activation function has a very significant advantage over the sigmoid function. The output of the sigmoid function lies in the range (0, 1) which means that if a strongly negative input is supplied to a sigmoid function, its output would be near zero. This could cause the same problem as discussed in the previous question. The neurons with negative inputs will get stuck in their current state and hence die.

But in case of tanh function, the output of a strongly negative input would be near -1 and only the zero-valued inputs would result in zero-valued outputs. Hence, the neurons with negative inputs would not get stuck during training.

15 Why is the softmax function used for the output layer?
In a neural network, the output variable is usually modeled as a probability distribution where the output nodes (the different values that the output variable can take) are mutually exclusive of each other. The softmax function is a generalization of the logistic function. It squashes the k-dimensional output variable into a

k-dimensional probability distribution where each entry is the probability of the output variable taking that value. Hence, each output node takes a value in the range (0, 1) and the sum of the values of all the entries is 1.

16 What is a good way to train a Deep Neural Network?

(a) Deep Neural Networks (DNNs) are mostly data hungry, so the more data you have, the better prediction you may get from them.

(b) Hidden units - Having more hidden units is still acceptable but if you have less than the optimal number of hidden units, then your model may suffer from underfitting.

(c) Use back-propagation with Rectified Linear Units.

(d) Always initialize the weights with small random numbers to break the symmetry between different units.

(e) You can try to use a gradually decreasing learning rate, which reduces after every epoch or few hundreds of instances, in order to speed up the convergence.

17 Name some of the regularization methods that could be used in Artificial Neural Networks.

Regularization is an approach used to prevent overfitting of a model. We have an entire section in this chapter where we will discuss it in detail.

Some of the ways to perform regularization in ANNs include:

(a) **Early Stopping** - It is an upper bound on the number of iterations to run before the model begins to overfit.

(b) **Dropout** - It is a technique in which you randomly drop units (along with their connections) from the neural network during training. This prevents the units from co-adapting too much and helps in reducing overfitting.

(c) **L1 or L2 penalty terms** - L1 or L2 are the regularization techniques which add an extra parameter λ to penalize the coefficients if they start overfitting.

18 What are autoencoders?

Autoencoders are ANNs which belong to Unsupervised Learning algorithms and are used to learn the encoding of the given dataset, typically for the purpose of Dimensionality Reduction. They consist of 2 parts:

(a) **encoding** (converting the higher dimensional input to a much lower dimension hidden layers)

(b) **decoding** (converting the hidden layers to the output).

Autoencoders try to learn the approximation to the input, and not actually predict any output. They are extremely useful as they find the low dimensional representation of the given dataset and also remove any redundancy present in it.

19 Describe Convolutional Neural Networks (CNNs).

CNNs are well suited for tasks such as image recognition or sequences in which the input has spatial structure. They are based on 4 building blocks:

(a) **Convolution** - The primary purpose of Convolution is to extract the features from the input image. A small matrix, known as filter or kernel, slides over the image and the dot product is computed. This dot product is called the Convolved Feature or Feature Map. By varying the filter, you can achieve different results such as Edge Detection, Blur, etc.

In practice, a CNN learns the values of these filters on its own during the training process. The more number of filters you have, the more image features get extracted and the better your network becomes at recognizing the patterns in the unseen images.

(b) **Rectified Linear Units** - The purpose of ReLU is to introduce nonlinearity, since most of the real-world data would be nonlinear. It is applied after every convolution step.

(c) **Pooling or Sub Sampling** - Spatial Pooling (also called downsampling) reduces the dimensionality of each feature map.

(d) **Classification (Fully Connected Layer)** - It is a traditional Multi-layer Perceptron. The term "Fully Connected" implies that every neuron in the previous layer is connected to every neuron in the next layer. The output from the convolution and pooling layers represent high-level features of the input image. The purpose of the Fully Connected layer is to use these features for classifying the input image into various classes based on the training dataset.

20 Tell me about Recurrent Neural Networks (RNNs).

The idea behind RNNs is to make use of the sequential information. They are called recurrent because they perform the same task for every element of a sequence, with the output being depended on the previous computations. They have shown great potential in various NLP tasks such as Speech Recognition, Image Captioning, Language Modeling etc.

Unlike traditional Neural Networks, RNNs have loops in them, allowing information to persist. Below figure shows a RNN being unrolled into a full network, which simply means writing out the network for the complete sequence, where x_i is the input at time i and h_i is the corresponding output. The output at time i depends on the previous information. For instance, predicting the next word in a sentence would depend on the words seen so far.

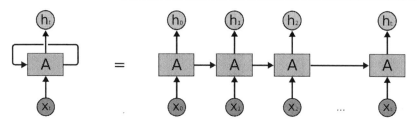

Figure 6.6: Recurrent Neural Network

21 Which one is better – random weights or same weights assignment to the units in the hidden layer?

The weights should be initialized with random values to ensure symmetry breaking (i.e. if all weights are the same, the hidden units will all represent the same thing). Typical initial weights are in the range of [-0.01, 0.01].

22 If the weights oscillate a lot over training iterations (often swinging between positive and negative values), what parameter do you need to tune to address this issue?

Learning Rate. If the learning rate is too high, it will cause the result to jump over the optimal point resulting in the weights oscillating between positive and negative. If it is too low, it may take a very long time to converge.

6.2 Regression

1 What is regression analysis?

Regression analysis is a set of statistical processes that estimate the relationship between the independent and dependent variables. The most common approach is to estimate the conditional expectation of the dependent variable given the independent variables (based on the assumption that the independent variables are linearly independent).

2 How does Regression belong to the Supervised Learning approach?

Regression belongs to the Supervised Learning category because it learns the model from the labeled dataset to predict the value of the continuous variables.

3 Name few types of regressions you are familiar with.

(a) Linear regression - It tries to fit a straight line to model the relationship between the dependent variable and the independent variable. It is used when the dependent variable is continuous.

(b) Logistic Regression - It finds the probability of success. It is used when the dependent variable is binary.

(c) Polynomial Regression - It fits a curve between dependent and independent variables, where the dependent variable is a polynomial function of the independent variable.

4 Explain the Bias-Variance trade-off.

Predictive models have a trade-off between the bias (how well does the model fit the data) and the variance (how much does the model change based on the changes in the inputs). Simpler models are stable (low variance) but they do not get close to the truth (high bias). More complex models are more prone to overfitting (high variance) but they are expressive enough to get close to the truth (low bias). The best model for a given problem usually lies somewhere in the middle.

5 What would you do if your model is suffering from low bias and high variance? And why?

Low bias occurs when the model's predicted values are near the actual values. In other words, the model becomes flexible enough to mimic the training data distribution. While it sounds like a great achievement, a flexible model has no generalization capabilities. It means when this model is tested on an unseen data, it would give poor results.

In such situations, you can use bagging algorithm (like Random Forest) to tackle high variance problem. Bagging algorithms divide a data set into subsets made with repeated randomized sampling. Then, these samples are used to generate a set of models using a single learning algorithm. Later, the model predictions are combined using voting (classification) or averaging (regression).

Also, to combat high variance, you can:
  (a) Use regularization technique, where the higher model coefficients get penalized, thereby lowering the model complexity.

  (b) Use top "n" features from the variable importance chart (Variable Importance is the statistical significance of each variable or feature in the data with respect to its effect on the generated model).

With all the variables in the dataset, the algorithm may be having difficulty in finding the meaningful signal.

6 Can you think of a scenario where a learning algorithm with low bias and high variance may be suitable?
Low bias and high variance can be used in K-Nearest Neighbors. They have low bias because they do not assume anything special about the data distribution and high variance because they can easily change their prediction in response to the composition of the training set.

7 What can you interpret from the coefficient estimates?
A regression equation can be written as:

$$Y = B_0 + \sum_{i=1}^{N}(B_iX_i) \qquad (6.20)$$

where B_0 is the intercept term and B_i is the coefficient for the predictor X_i.
  (a) Intercept - It can be interpreted as the predicted value for the response variable when all the predictor values are 0.

  (b) Coefficients for Continuous predictors - For all the continuous predictors X_i, their corresponding coefficient B_i represents the difference in the response variable's predicted value for each one unit difference in X_i keeping all other X_j constant.

  (c) Coefficients for Categorical predictors - For all the categorical predictors X_i, since they can be coded as 0,1,2 etc., a one unit difference in X_i represents switching from one category to the other, keeping all other X_j constant.

```
from sklearn import linear_model
import numpy as np

# Let's use our same training dataset of sum of 2 integers.
input_data = np.random.randint(50, size=(20, 2))
input_sum = np.zeros(len(input_data))
for row in range(len(input_data)):
    input_sum[row] = input_data[row][0] + input_data[row][1]

# Let's build a simple Linear Regression model
regression_model = linear_model.LinearRegression()
regression_model.fit(input_data, input_sum)

# As you would expect, the coefficients of the inputs
```

```
# should be 1 and intercept 0.
print("Model Coefficients are " + str(regression_model.coef_)
    )
print("Model Intercept is " + str(regression_model.intercept_
    ))

# Since, we had fit_intercept term as True in our model,
# we get a very small, close to 0 value for it.
# Let's see what happens when we set it to False
regression_model = linear_model.LinearRegression(
    fit_intercept=False)
regression_model.fit(input_data, input_sum)
print("Model Coefficients are " + str(regression_model.coef_)
    )
print("Model Intercept is " + str(regression_model.intercept_
    ))
```

8 What do you mean by overfitting a regression model? What are the ways to avoid it?

Overfitting a regression model occurs when you attempt to estimate too many parameters from a sample that is too small. If the sample size isn't large enough, then you won't be able to fit a model that adequately approximates the true model for the response variable.

Cross-validation can detect overfitted models by determining how well your model generalizes to other datasets by partitioning the data.

To avoid overfitting in the first place, you should try to get a large enough sample. You can also use various regularization terms such as L1 or L2 regularization.

9 What are the downfalls of using too many or too few variables for performing regression?

Too many variables can cause overfitting. If you have too many variables in your regression model, then your model may suffer from lack of degree of freedom and have some variable correlated to each other.

Having too few variables, on the other hand, will lead to underfitting as you won't have enough predictors to learn the training dataset.

10 What is linear regression? Why is it called linear?

In linear regression, the dependent variable y is the linear combination of the parameters. For instance, if x is the independent variable, and β_0 and β_1 be 2 parameters.

$$y = \beta_0 + \beta_1 x \tag{6.21}$$

Note that instead of x, you can have any function of x, such as x^2. In that case,

$$y = \beta_0 + \beta_1 x^2 \tag{6.22}$$

CRACKING THE MACHINE LEARNING INTERVIEW

This is still a linear regression as y is still a linear combination of the parameters (β_0 and β_1).

11 How can you check if the regression model fits the data well?

You can use the following statistics to test the model's fitness:

(a) R-squared - It is a statistical measure of how close the data points are to the fitted regression line.

(b) F-test - It evaluates the null hypothesis that all regression coefficients are equal to zero versus the alternative hypothesis that at least one is not. It is used to identify the best model which fits the given dataset.

(c) Root Mean Square Error (RMSE) - It is the square root of the variance of the residuals. It measures the average deviation of the estimates from the observed value.

12 What is a limitation of R-squared? How do you address it?

R-squared ranges between 0 and 1, with 0 indicating that the proposed model does not improve prediction over the mean model and 1 indicating the perfect prediction. One drawback of R-squared is that it can only increase as the predictors are added to the regression model, even if they are not actually improving the model's fit.

To address this issue, you use Adjusted R-squared for models where the number of predictors is greater than 1. Adjusted R-squared incorporates the model's degrees of freedom and decreases if the increase in model fit does not make up for the loss of degrees of freedom. So, it only increases when the model fit is actually improved.

13 When would you use k-Nearest Neighbors for regression?

You can use K-NN in regression for estimating the continuous variables. One of the algorithms is using a weighted average of the k nearest neighbors, weighted by the inverse of their distance:

(a) Compute the Euclidean distance from the test instance to the labeled instances.

(b) Order the labeled instances by increasing distance.

(c) Find a heuristically optimal k nearest neighbors, based on RMSE.

(d) Calculate an inverse distance weighted average with the k-nearest multivariate neighbors.

```
from sklearn import neighbors
import numpy as np
import matplotlib.pyplot as plt

# Let's create a small random dataset
np.random.seed(0)
X = 15 * np.random.rand(50, 1)
y = 5 * np.random.rand(50, 1)
X_test = [[1], [3], [5], [7], [9], [11], [13]]
```

```
# We will use k=5 in our example and try different
# weights for our model.
n_neighbors = 5
weights = ['uniform', 'distance']
for i, weight in enumerate(weights):
    knn_regressor = neighbors.KNeighborsRegressor(
                                    n_neighbors=
                                        n_neighbors,
                                    weights=weight)
    knn_regressor.fit(X, y)
    y_pred = knn_regressor.predict(X_test)
    plt.subplot(2, 1, i + 1)
    plt.scatter(X, y, c='r', label='data')
    plt.scatter(X_test, y_pred, c='g', label='prediction')
    plt.legend()
    plt.title("KNeighborsRegressor (k = %i, weights = '%s')"
        %
                                    (n_neighbors,
                                        weights[i]))

plt.show()
```

14 Do you always need the intercept term? When do you need it and when do you not?

The intercept term signifies the response variable's shift from the origin. It ensures that the model would be unbiased, i.e., the residual mean is 0. If you omit the intercept term, then your model is forced to go through the origin and the slope would become steeper (and biased).

Hence, you should not remove the intercept term unless you are completely sure that it is 0. For instance, if you are calculating the area of a rectangle, with height and width as the predictor variables, you can omit the intercept term since you know that the area should be 0 when both height and width are 0.

15 What do you mean by collinearity?

Collinearity is a phenomenon in which two predictor variables are linearly related to each other. Let X_1 and X_2 be two variables, then:

$$X_1 = \lambda_0 + \lambda_1 X_2, \tag{6.23}$$

where λ_0 and λ_1 are constants. X_1 and X_2 would be perfectly collinear if λ_0 is 0.

16 Explain multicollinearity.

Multicollinearity is a phenomenon in regression where one predictor (independent variable x_i) can be predicted as a linear combination of other predictors with a significant accuracy.

$$\lambda_0 + \lambda_1 X_1 + \lambda_2 X_2 + ... + \lambda_k X_k = 0 \tag{6.24}$$

The issue with perfect multicollinearity is that it makes $X^T X$ non-invertible, which is used by the Ordinary Least Squares to find the optimal estimates. So, you would need to remove the redundant features and then perform Ordinary Least Squares (OLS).

OLS is a method for estimating the unknown parameters in a linear regression model, by minimizing the sum of the squares of the differences between the observed and predicted response variable.

17 What are the assumptions that standard linear regression models with the standard estimation techniques make?
The standard linear regression model makes the following assumptions:
  (a) A linear relationship between the parameters and the response variable.

  (b) The residuals follow the normal distribution. [A residual, e_i, is the difference between the predicted value and the true value of corresponding dependent (response) variable, y_i, where i represents the specific example in the data.]

  (c) No perfect multicollinearity among the predictors.

  (d) The number of observations is greater than the number of predictors.

  (e) The mean of residuals is zero.

6.3 Regularization

1 What is Regularization?

Regularization refers to the approach of avoiding overfitting by penalizing the coefficient terms. Sometimes you want to optimize two competing things simultaneously. For instance, you want to minimize the area of a rectangle, let's denote it by $a(x)$ while maximizing its perimeter, $p(x)$, where x is the input vector of height and width. So, your regularization problem can be written as:

$$min_x(a(x) + \lambda \frac{1}{p(x)}),$$ (6.25)

where λ is the regularization term or regularizer which penalizes the smaller value of $p(x)$. Decision Tree pruning is a classic example of regularization.

2 When does Regularization become necessary in Machine Learning?

Regularization becomes important when the model begins to either overfit or underfit. Another scenario where it is useful to have regularization is when you want to optimize two competing functions simultaneously. In that case, there is a trade-off between them and a regularization/penalty term is used to optimize the more important function at the cost of the less important one.

3 What do you understand by Ridge Regression? Why do you need it? How is it different from Ordinary Least Squares (OLS) Regression?

Ridge Regression is a statistical technique used for analyzing multiple regression data which suffer from multicollinearity. When multicollinearity occurs, least squares estimates become unbiased and lead to overdetermined (over-fitted) system of equations. Unfortunately, their variances can be so large that they may actually be far from the true value. Ridge regression adds a degree of bias to the regression estimates thereby reducing the standard errors.

In OLS, the regression coefficients are estimated as:

$$\beta = (X^TX)^{-1}X^TY$$ (6.26)

Ridge regression adds a penalty term, λ, to the diagonal entries of the term X^TX. Adding a penalty term reduces overfitting and guarantees a solution. The equation for ridge regression is given as:

$$Y(\beta) = ||Y - X\beta||_2^2 + \lambda||\beta||_2^2$$ (6.27)

The resulting regression estimates are:

$$\beta = (X^TX + \lambda I)^{-1}X^TY$$ (6.28)

Therefore, Ridge regression puts further constraints on the parameters β_js. Even if X^TX becomes singular, adding λI to it effectively adds λ to each eigenvalue, so the result is always invertible. And hence, optimal β will always exist. Instead of just minimizing the residual sum of squares, you also have a penalty term on β. With an appropriate λ, the mean squared error of ridge regression would be less than that of OLS.

4 What is Lasso Regression? How is it different from OLS?

Lasso (Least Absolute Shrinkage and Selection Operator) minimizes the sum of the square of errors by putting a constraint on the sum of the absolute values of the coefficients. Therefore, the best way to minimize the sum of absolute values of the coefficients is to make less relevant ones zero. In this way, Lasso can be used to select the important features. The equation for Lasso regression is given as:

$$Y(\beta) = ||Y - X\beta||_2^2 + \lambda ||\beta||_1 \qquad (6.29)$$

5 How does Ridge regression differ from Lasso regression?

Both of them are regularization techniques, with the difference in their penalty functions. The penalty in Ridge regression is the sum of the squares of the coefficients whereas, for the Lasso, it is the sum of the absolute values of the coefficients. The Lasso regression is used to achieve sparse solutions by making some of the coefficients zero. The Ridge regression, on the other hand, tries to smoothen the solution as it keeps all the coefficients but minimizes the sum of their squares.

6 Why does LASSO (L-1) produce solutions with zero-valued coefficients as opposed to Ridge Regression (L-2)?

A standard LASSO regularization problem looks like:

$$min_x ||y - Ax||^2 + \lambda ||x||_1 \qquad (6.30)$$

For the sake of simplicity, let us consider a 2-D space. Figure 6.7 shows how an L-1 norm ball would look in 2-D:

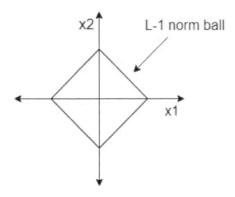

Figure 6.7: L-1 norm ball

The optimal solution for least squares problem would be $y = Ax$, but by adding the regularization, the optimal x may result in $y - Ax = b$, which is another line parallel to $y = Ax$. If you draw these parallel lines on the same figure as the L-1 norm ball, you would notice that the intersection of that line with L-1 ball occurs at one of the axes as shown in Figure 6.8. This means, that the coefficient for the other variable is 0.

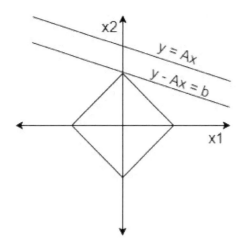

Figure 6.8: L-1 norm ball with Least squares solution

Extending the same concept to a larger space, it implies that some of the coefficients would be 0 in the L-1 regularization solution.

Let's draw the same lines along with L-2 norm ball (ridge regression). You can notice in Figure 6.9 that the intersection (optimal solution) occurs when you draw a perpendicular from the origin to the line, resulting in a smooth solution with non-zero coefficients.

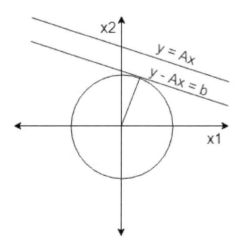

Figure 6.9: L-2 norm ball with Least squares solution

CRACKING THE MACHINE LEARNING INTERVIEW

7 What is the difference between the L-1 and L-2 regularization?

L-1 regularization minimizes the sum of absolute errors and is thus, used for feature selection in sparse feature space by making few coefficients zero. L-2 regularization, on the other hand, minimizes the sum of squares of absolute errors and is used to smoothen the solution by creating small distributed coefficients.

L-1 is more robust since it is resistant to the outliers. L-2 squares the error, so for any outlier, its square term would be huge.

L-2 produces a unique solution, since there is only single shortest distance between two points whereas, in case of L-1, you may have multiple solutions.

This page

intentionally

left blank

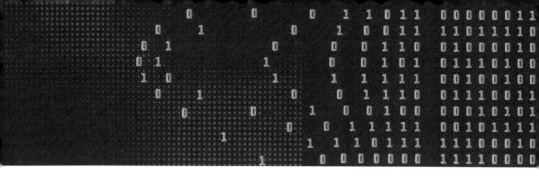

7. Unsupervised Learning

Unsupervised Learning is another very popular class of Machine Learning, extensively used to find

1. Clusters of the data,
2. Low-dimensional representations of the data,
3. Interesting coordinates and correlations among the data instances, and
4. Interesting directions in the data.

For instance, learning human behavior and trying to group individuals based on the common behavior is an Unsupervised Learning task. The recommendation system is a classic example of Unsupervised Learning which recommends the products based on what the users have liked before. Anomaly Detection is another type of this field which is used in almost every medium to large scale company to carry out various tasks such as Fraud detection, system health monitoring, etc.

All these examples try to find the common patterns in the dataset and group similar items together. They do not have any notion of a class label which tags the data. This is what Unsupervised Learning is.

The two most important areas of Unsupervised Learning which are frequently asked in the interviews are Clustering and Dimensionality Reduction. Let's discuss both of them in detail now.

7.1 Clustering

1 Why and where do you need to use Cluster analysis?

Cluster analysis is the task of grouping (clustering) a set of objects in such a way that objects in the same cluster are much more similar to each other than to those in the other clusters. In some cases, Cluster analysis can be used for the initial analysis of the given dataset based on the different target attributes.

For the data lacking the output labels, you can use clustering technique to automatically find the class labels by grouping the input data instances into different clusters and then assigning a unique label to each cluster. Cluster analysis has been found useful in a wide variety of applications such as weather forecast, customer segmentation for marketing, Information Retrieval, genetic study etc.

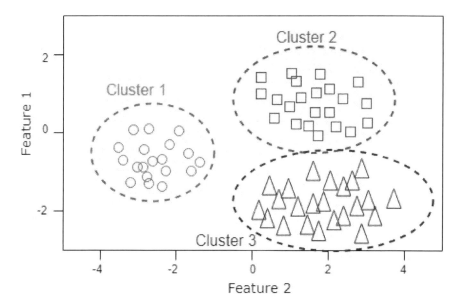

Figure 7.1: Sample Clustering

```
# Scikit-Learn provides 'cluster' module to use
# clustering algorithms.
# In this example, we will use simple KMeans Clustering model
    .

from sklearn.cluster import KMeans
import numpy as np
import matplotlib.pyplot as plt

# Let's create our sample dataset for training
data = np.zeros((60, 2))
data[0:20, 0] = np.random.uniform(-3.5, -1.5, size=20)
data[0:20, 1] = np.random.uniform(-1, 0, size=20)

data[20:40, 0] = np.random.uniform(0, 4, size=20)
data[20:40, 1] = np.random.uniform(-3, -1, size=20)
```

```
data[40:60, 0] = np.random.uniform(0, 3, size=20)
data[40:60, 1] = np.random.uniform(0, 2, size=20)

# We have number of clusters=3
kmeans_model = KMeans(n_clusters=3)
kmeans_model.fit(data)

# Let's plot our training dataset with cluster
# labels assigned by our KMeans model
colors = ['red', 'green', 'blue']
for i in range(len(data)):
    # let's get the color from model's label
    cluster_label = kmeans_model.labels_[i]

    # Now, plot the point with corresponding
    # color for the label
    plt.scatter(data[i][0], data[i][1],
                color=colors[cluster_label])

plt.show()
```

2 Give examples of some of the Cluster analysis methods.

Some of the most widely used Clustering methods are:

(a) Hierarchical Clustering - It produces a hierarchy of clusters, either by merging smaller clusters into larger ones or dividing the larger clusters into smaller ones.

The merging or splitting of clusters depends on the metric used for measuring the dissimilarity between the sets of data instances. Some of the commonly used metrics are Euclidean distance, Manhattan distance, Hamming distance etc.

(b) K-means Clustering - It assigns the data points to k clusters such that each data point belongs to the cluster with the closest mean. It is suitable for large number of data-points and uses far lesser iterations than the Hierarchical Clustering.

3 Differentiate between Partitioning method and Hierarchical method.

(a) A partitional clustering is a division of the set of data objects into non-overlapping clusters such that each object is in exactly one cluster whereas a hierarchical clustering is a set of nested clusters which are organized as a tree.

(b) Hierarchical clustering does not require any input parameters, whereas the partitional clustering algorithms require the number of clusters to begin.

(c) Partitional clustering is generally faster than hierarchical clustering.

4 Explain K-Means Clustering and its objective.
K-Means Clustering is a technique used for handling a large number of data points. It partitions the dataset into k clusters such that each data point belongs to the cluster with the nearest mean.

K-Means Clustering starts from some initial clusters and then reassigns the data points to k clusters to minimize the total penalty term. The centroid of each cluster is used as the new mean and the whole assignment process is repeated until there is no further change in the data points assignment. This is a versatile algorithm used to find groups in the unlabeled dataset.

5 How do you evaluate the quality of the clusters that are generated by a run of k-Means?
One of the ways to evaluate the clusters' quality is to resample the data (via bootstrap or by adding small noise) and compute the closeness of the resulting partitions, measured by Jaccard similarity. This approach allows you to estimate the frequency with which similar clusters can be recovered after resampling.

The mathematical formula for calculating the Jaccard similarity coefficient is given as:

$$J(A,B) = \frac{|A \cap B|}{|A \cup B|}, \qquad (7.1)$$

where A and B are two sample sets. The coefficient is simply the total number of elements common in both the sample sets divided by the total number of elements which are present either in A or B or both.

6 How do you select k for K-Means Clustering algorithm?
There is no hard and fast rule to select the optimal value of "k". In the absence of any a priori set of categories, you would want to minimize "k" while also minimizing the average cluster variance at the same time. A simple approach is to plot the number of clusters vs the average cluster variance and choose the value of k where adding more clusters does not have a significant impact on the cluster variance.

7 How would you assess the quality of the Clustering technique?
Cluster evaluation is a hard problem and most of the times, there is no perfect solution to it. Otherwise, it would be a classification problem where each cluster represents one class. The common assessment approaches involve:

(a) Internal Evaluation, where the clustering result is compared with the found clusters and their relationship with each other.

(b) External Evaluation, where the result of the clustering is compared to an existing "ground truth". However, obtaining an external reference result is not straightforward in most of the cases.

(c) Manual Evaluation by a human expert.

(d) Indirect Evaluation by evaluating the utility of the clustering in its intended application.

7.2 Dimensionality Reduction

1 What is Dimensionality Reduction and why do you need it?

As the name suggests, Dimensionality Reduction means finding a lower-dimensional representation of the dataset such that the original dataset is preserved as much as possible even after reducing the number of dimensions. Dimensionality Reduction reduces the time and storage space required. And removal of multi-collinearity improves the performance of the Machine Learning model.

Many high dimensional datasets such as videos, human genes, etc. are difficult to process as is. For such data, you need to remove the unnecessary and redundant features and keep only the most informative ones to better learn from them.

2 Are Dimensionality Reduction techniques Supervised or Unsupervised?

In general, you use Dimensionality Reduction technique for Unsupervised Learning tasks. But, they can also be used in Supervised Learning.

One of the standard methods of Supervised Dimensionality Reduction is called Linear Discriminant Analysis (LDA). It is designed to find low-dimensional projection that maximizes the class separation.

Another approach is partial least squares (PLS), which looks for the projections having the highest covariance with the group labels.

3 Tell me some of the ways of reducing the dimensionality of the given dataset.

There are a lot of techniques for reducing the number of dimensions in a dataset. Some of them include:

(a) Principal Component Analysis (PCA) - In PCA, the features are transformed into a new set of features (much lesser than the original), which are linear combination of the original features.

(b) Backward Feature Elimination - In this method, you start with all the n dimensions and eliminate each of them one by one. The one with the smallest increase in the sum of square of error (SSR), would be removed, leaving n-1 input features. This process is repeated until no feature can be further removed.

(c) Forward Feature Selection method - In this method, you select one feature and analyze the performance of the model by adding another feature. Here, the selection of a feature is based on the larger improvement in the model's performance.

(d) Linear discriminant analysis (LDA) - discussed above in the previous question.

(e) Generalized discriminant analysis (GDA) - The conventional LDA is not suitable for non-linear dataset. For such cases, you use Generalized discriminant analysis which deals with the nonlinear discriminant analysis using the kernel function operator.

4 **What do you mean by Curse of Dimensionality?**

When the number of features is very large relative to the number of instances in the dataset, certain Machine Learning algorithms struggle to train effective models. This problem of having a huge feature space is known as the Curse of Dimensionality.

5 **Is feature selection a Dimensionality Reduction technique?**

The feature selection is a special case of Dimensionality Reduction in which the set of features made by feature selection must be a subset of the original feature set, whereas it is not necessary in Dimensionality Reduction, in general (for instance PCA reduces the dimensionality by making new synthetic features from the linear combination of the original ones).

6 **How would you reduce the dimensionality of a dataset which has correlated features?**

You can calculate the correlation matrix, using the linear correlation node. Linear Correlation node calculates the correlation coefficient for all the pairs of numerical columns in the dataset, as the Pearson's Product Moment Coefficient, and for all pairs of nominal columns, as the Pearson's chi square value. You can use it to build the correlation matrix for the features, and for all the pairs of columns with correlation higher than a given threshold, remove one of the two features.

7 **What are the problems with a large feature space? How does it affect the computational complexity?**

As we discussed earlier, a large feature space leads to the Curse of Dimensionality, which negatively impacts the prediction capability of the model. As you keep increasing the number of features, the dimensionality of the feature space becomes more sparse. And, it becomes easier to find a separating hyperplane, which can cause overfitting since the learned model would work very well on the training dataset but poorly when fed the test dataset. The runtime complexity generally grows exponentially with the increase in the number of dimensions.

8 **What is the difference between density-sparse data and dimensionally-sparse data?**

Density sparse data means that a high percentage of the data contains 0 or null values. Dimensionally sparse data is the one which has a large feature space, in which some of the features are redundant, correlated etc.

9 **Is it beneficial to perform dimensionality reduction before fitting an SVM? Why or why not?**

Reducing the number of features will definitely reduce the computational complexity of the model but it may not improve the performance of SVM, because SVM already uses regularization to avoid over-fitting. So, performing Dimensionality Reduction before SVM may not improve the performance of the SVM classifier.

10 **Suppose you have a very sparse matrix with highly dimensional rows. Is projecting these rows on a random vector of relatively small dimensionality a**

valid dimensionality reduction technique?

Although it may not sound intuitive, but random projection is a valid dimensionality reduction method. It is a computationally efficient way to reduce the dimensionality by trading a controlled amount of error for smaller model sizes and faster processing times. Random projection is based on the idea that if the data points in a sparse feature space have a very high dimension, then you can project them into a lower dimensional space in a way that preserves the pairwise distances between the points approximately.

11 What is Principal Component Analysis?

PCA is a Dimensionality Reduction technique that transforms a high dimensional feature space into smaller components which still retain most of the relevant information. The components are such that the first component has the maximum variance in the data, followed by the second component and so on with the constraint that all the components are orthogonal to each other.

12 What do you mean by Independent Component Analysis? What is the difference between Independent Component Analysis (ICA) and Principal Component Analysis (PCA)?

ICA is a statistical technique in Unsupervised Learning which decomposes a multi-variate signal into independent non-Gaussian components. It defines a generative model in which the data variables are assumed to be linear or nonlinear mixtures of some unknown latent variables, and the mixing system is also unknown. The latent variables are assumed to be non-Gaussian and mutually independent, and they are called the independent components of the observed data. These independent components are found by ICA. You can use ICA for Facial Recognition, Stock Prediction etc.

PCA helps to find a low-rank representation of the dataset such that the first vector of the PCA is the one that best explains the variability of your data (the principal direction), the second vector is the 2nd best explanation and is orthogonal to the first one, and so on.

ICA finds a representation of the dataset as independent sub-elements. You can think of the data as a mixed signal, consisting of independent vectors.

13 What is Fisher Discriminant Analysis? How is it different from PCA? Is it Supervised or not?

Fisher Discriminant Analysis is a Supervised Learning technique, which tries to find the components in such a way that the class separation is maximized while minimizing the within class variance.

Both Principal Component Analysis and Fisher Discriminant Analysis techniques are used for feature reduction by finding the eigenvalues and eigenvectors to project the existing the feature space into new dimensions. The major difference between them is that PCA falls under Unsupervised Learning and tries to find the components such that the variance in the complete dataset is maximized whereas Fisher Discriminant Analysis, as described earlier, tries to maximize the separation between the classes.

14 What are the differences between Factor Analysis and Principal Component Analysis (PCA)?

PCA involves transforming the given data into a smaller set of components such that they are linearly uncorrelated to each other. Factor analysis is a generalization of PCA which is based on the maximum-likelihood.

Factor Analysis is used when you want to test a theoretical model of latent factors causing observed variables. And PCA is used when you want to simply reduce your correlated observed variables to a smaller set of important independent orthogonal variables.

15 How is Singular Value Decomposition (SVD) mathematically related to EVD for PCA?

PCA is usually performed using Eigenvalue Decomposition but you can also use Singular Value Decomposition to perform PCA. Let's say that you have an input data X of size n X p, where n is the number of observations and p is the number of features. And for the sake of simplicity, let's assume that X is already centered, i.e the column means are zeros.

So, the Covariance matrix C is of size p X p and is given by:

$$C = \frac{X^T X}{n-1} \tag{7.2}$$

Let L be the diagonal matrix with eigenvalues λ_i and V the matrix of eigenvectors.

Since C is a symmetric matrix, you can diagonalize it as:

$$C = VLV^T, \tag{7.3}$$

Now, SVD of X is given by:

$$X = USV^T, \tag{7.4}$$

where S is the diagonal matrix with singular values s_i. Putting the SVD of X in equation 7.2, you get:

$$C = \frac{(USV^T)^T(USV^T)}{n-1}$$
$$= \frac{VSU^TUSV^T}{n-1} \tag{7.5}$$
$$= V\frac{S^2}{n-1}V^T$$

Comparing equations 7.3 and 7.5, you can see that the eigenvalues are related to the singular values via

$$\lambda_i = \frac{s_i^2}{n-1} \tag{7.6}$$

16 Why do you need to center the data for PCA and what can happen if you do not do it?
Centering the data means bringing the mean to the origin, by subtracting it from the data. It is required to ensure that the first principal component is indeed in the direction of maximum variance. A centered data (zero mean) is used to find a basis which minimizes the mean squared error. If you do not perform centering then the first component might instead be misguiding and correspond to the mean of the data.

Centering is not required if you are performing PCA on a correlation matrix, since the data would already be centered after calculating the correlations.

17 Do you need to normalize the data for PCA? Why or why not?
PCA is about transforming the given data to the space which maximizes the variance. If the dataset is not normalized then PCA may select some feature with the highest variance in the original dataset making it more important. For instance, if you use "grams" for a feature instead of "kgs", then its variance would increase and PCA might think that it has more impact, which may not be correct. Hence, it is very important to normalize the data for PCA.

18 Is rotation necessary in PCA? Why or why not?
Yes, the rotation (orthogonality) is necessary because it maximizes the difference between the variance captured by the components, making them easier to interpret. The rotation only changes the actual coordinates of the points and not the relative location of the components. Without the rotation, you will have to select more number of components thereby belittling the effect of PCA.

19 Is PCA a linear model or not? Explain.
PCA projects the original dataset into a lower dimensional linear subspace, called hyperplane. All the mappings, rotations and transformations performed are linear and can be expressed in terms of linear algebraic operations. Thus, a PCA is a linear method for Dimensionality Reduction.

20 Have you heard of Kernel PCA or other non-linear Dimensionality Reduction techniques? Can you explain any one of them?
A Kernel PCA is an extension of a linear PCA, in the sense that it uses kernel methods to perform PCA. Let's assume that your dataset has n points. Now, in general, it is not always possible to linearly separate them in d dimensions if $d < n$, but you can almost always linearly separate them if $d \geq n$. So, you take a function ϕ, which maps the data points to n dimension.

$$\phi : R^d -> R^n \tag{7.7}$$

A kernel function is defined as:

$$K = k(\mathbf{x}, \mathbf{y}) = (\phi(\mathbf{x}), \phi(\mathbf{y})) = \phi(\mathbf{x})^T \phi(\mathbf{y}) \tag{7.8}$$

Instead of calculating ϕ explicitly, you use the kernel method to directly map the input space into a higher dimension in which the data points are linearly separable.

21 What Dimensionality Reduction techniques can be used for preprocessing the data?

Dimensionality Reduction can be broadly divided into Feature Extraction and Feature Selection, both of which are used for preprocessing the data. The resulting dataset is then used for learning purpose.

22 What is the difference between Feature Selection and Feature Extraction?

Both of these techniques are used to avoid the Curse of Dimensionality, simplify the models by removing redundant and irrelevant features, and reduce overfitting. But the difference lies in the way they achieve it.

Feature selection means selecting a subset of features from the given features, based on some criteria. Some of the ways to perform Feature Selection are Forward Selection and Backward Elimination. And Feature extraction means projecting the given feature space into a new feature space, such as in SVD and PCA.

23 What are some of the Feature extraction techniques used for Dimensionality Reduction?

Some of the Feature Extraction methods used for reducing the dataset dimensionality are:
  (a) Independent Component Analysis (ICA)
  (b) Principal Component Analysis (PCA)
  (c) Kernel Based PCA
  (d) Singular Value Decomposition (SVD)

This page

intentionally

left blank

8. Data Preprocessing

It is fair to assume that the real world data would be noisy, inconsistent and/or have missing values. This makes it extremely important to perform some kind of data preprocessing before feeding the data directly to the Machine Learning algorithm. From a developer's point of view, Data Preprocessing is generally the most time consuming step in the complete Machine Learning pipeline.

Data Preprocessing involves the following steps in order:

1. Data cleaning: Cleaning the raw data consists of filling the missing values, removing noise from it and correcting the inconsistent data.

2. Data Integration: Putting together the data from various sources.

3. Data transformation: Normalizing, Aggregating and constructing the new feature space based on the existing features.

4. Data reduction: This step reduces the number of features by removing unnecessary, less relevant and/or correlated features using Dimensionality Reduction techniques. It also performs sampling to reduce the total number of examples to be fed into the training process.

Now, let's delve into the salient interview questions covering various aspects of Data Preprocessing.

1 Explain Feature Selection and its importance.

Feature Selection is a process of selecting a subset of relevant features from the given ones. Some learning methods, such as k-NN and Naive Bayes, are sensitive to irrelevant or redundant features. Feature Selection can be extremely useful in such learning models. It simplifies the model by reducing the number of parameters, decreases the training time and avoids the Curse of Dimensionality.

2 What do you understand by variance threshold approach?

The variance threshold approach is a simple baseline approach used for Feature Selection. It is motivated by the idea that low variance implies a less significant feature and hence, it removes all the features whose variances do not meet some threshold. By default, it removes all the features that have the same value in all samples, i.e all zero-variance features. Since the variance threshold method considers only the features and not the outputs, you can use it in Unsupervised Learning problems.

3 Tell me some of the Feature Selection methods.

There are various ways to select the relevant features in a dataset. Some of them include:

(a) Forward Selection - In this method, you keep adding a feature which best improves your model until the addition of a new feature does not improve the performance of the model.

(b) Backward Elimination - In this method, you keep removing a feature from the complete set, which best improves your model until the removal of a feature does not improve the performance of the model.

(c) Recursive Feature Elimination - It is a greedy approach which repeatedly creates models and keeps aside the best or the worst performing feature in each iteration. It constructs the next model with the left features until all the features are exhausted. It then ranks the features based on the order of their elimination.

4 What are some of the good Feature Selection approaches that do not involve exhaustive search?

(a) Forward Selection - It is efficient for choosing a small subset of the features, but misses features whose usefulness requires other features (feature synergy).

(b) Backward Elimination - It is efficient for discarding a small subset of the features and it preserves the features whose usefulness requires other features.

Both of them use the Hill Climbing approach. Hill Climbing is an iterative optimization technique which begins with an arbitrary initial state and attempts to improve the solution incrementally. The process is repeated till the new state results in a better solution than the previous one. If there is no better solution, the process stops. Since Hill Climbing approach tries to find the best move for the immediate step only, it generally results in a solution which is a local optimum, which would be the global optima in case of the convex problems.

5 Is there any negative impact of using too many or too few variables for training a model?

As mentioned earlier, having too many or too few variables can negatively affect the model's performance. Too many variables can cause overfitting as your model may have some variables correlated to each other.

Having too few variables, on the other hand, can lead to underfitting as you won't have enough variables to learn the training dataset correctly.

6 Is there any optimal number of features that should be used for learning?

In general, there is no formula to calculate the optimal number of features that should be used for training. There are a couple of techniques which you can apply. If you already know the dataset and know which features are relevant, then you can manually configure your model. Otherwise, you can learn a model to decide the best features for your dataset. Based on either the processing time or the model's accuracy threshold, you can create a set of learned models and finally use the one which performs better than the others.

7 Do you think using a particular model for training can affect the choice of a Feature Selection method?

A Feature Selection step is performed before learning a model for the training dataset. So, in general, a model does not force you into using a specific Feature Selection approach. The only way it can affect the Feature Selection is the model's restriction on what kind of features it can use. For instance, if a model can only learn numerical data, then you either do not select a categorical feature or you need to transform it before feeding it to your model. This step is known as Feature Transformation or Feature Engineering.

8 What do you understand by Feature Engineering?

Feature Engineering is the process of using domain knowledge of the data to transform the raw data into features that make Machine Learning algorithms work. The process of Feature Engineering includes deciding on the features, testing the model's accuracy with those features, and if needed, improving the features. With good features, you can get great results even with less optimal models.

This page

intentionally

left blank

9. Model Evaluation

Model Evaluation is an integral part of the Machine Learning pipeline and is used to assess the accuracy or performance of the trained model. If the trained model looks good, you can deploy it to run it on the new test data. Otherwise, you need to retrain your model to improve its performance.

There are two methods of evaluating the models, viz. Hold-Out and Cross-Validation. In order to avoid overfitting, both of these methods use a test dataset to evaluate the model's performance.

1. Hold-Out: In this method, the dataset is randomly divided into three subsets:
    (a) Training set: It is used to build the predictive models.

    (b) Validation set: It is used to fine-tune the model's parameters and select the best performing model.

    (c) Test set: It is the actual dataset on which you need the trained model to perform better.

    If the model performs better on the training set than the test set, it means that it is probably suffering from overfitting.

2. Cross-Validation: It is another approach to achieve an unbiased estimate of the model's performance. In k-fold cross-validation, you divide the dataset into k equal sized subsets and build k different models. For each model, you leave one subset from the set as the test set and remaining k-1 are used as the training set.

Now, let's discuss some of the most frequently asked questions from this topic.

1 How do you measure the model's accuracy?

There are various ways to measure the accuracy of a model such as AUROC curve, Precision-Recall curve, F-Test, t-test etc. All of these techniques have been explained in detail earlier in "General Machine Learning Questions" and "Supervised Learning" chapters.

2 What would you do if the training results in very low accuracy?

If the model is not doing anything better than random choice, then either there is no connection between the features and the class, or your classifier is not apt for the given dataset. You should also check if your model is suffering from high bias or high variance problem. You can also test if there is any correlation between the features and try to either use cross validation or remove the outliers/redundant features.

3 Name some of the evaluation metrics you know of. Something apart from accuracy?

(a) Logarithmic loss (or logloss) evaluates the predictions of probabilities of membership to a given class.

(b) Area under ROC curve (AUROC).

(c) Mean Squared Error (MSE) or Mean Absolute Error, used in Regression.

4 How do you know if your model is overfitting?

A simple way to check whether the model overfits is to measure the error on the training and test datasets. If the error on training dataset is low and high on test and/or validation dataset, then there likely is overfitting in the model. As you can

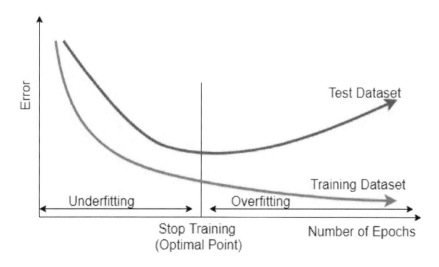

Figure 9.1: Error varying with Number of Epochs

see in Figure 9.1, if you keep improving the training set's accuracy, then beyond the optimal point, the model starts to overfit and the test set's accuracy starts decreasing (the error rate starts increasing). However, if you stop training early, then your model might underfit and not learn from the training set completely.

5 How do you ensure that you are not overfitting a model?
There are three main methods to avoid overfitting:

(a) Keep the model simple: reduce the variance by taking into account fewer variables and parameters, thereby removing some of the noise in the training data.

(b) Use cross-validation: It performs multiple splitting of the dataset into training and test dataset, trains a model for each one of them and selects the best learned model with least error or highest accuracy on the test dataset.

(c) Use regularization techniques such as LASSO or Ridge regression which penalize certain model parameters if they are likely to cause overfitting.

6 How do you assess the results of a Logistic Regression model?
There are many ways to evaluate the Logistic Regression model. You can use Likelihood test, which compares the likelihood of the data under the full model against the likelihood of the data under a model with fewer predictors. You can also use k-fold cross validation.

Another approach is AIC, the measure of fit which penalizes the model for the number of model coefficients. Thus, the model with minimum AIC value is always preferred.

7 Which is better: too many false positives or too many false negatives?
It depends on the underlying problem being solved. For instance, if you are trying to predict a disease, then having a false positive may be better than a false negative, where you would want to be preventive than predicting that the disease is not present whereas, in reality, it is.

On the other hand, if you are doing spam filtering, then you would be okay by not marking a spam email as spam (false negative) but having a false positive, i.e, marking an important email as spam might be very dangerous as it may never get delivered to the user due to spam filtering. In that case, having a false negative is better than false positive.

8 Define Precision and Recall.
Precision is the fraction of relevant instances among the retrieved instances, whereas recall is the fraction of relevant instances that have been retrieved over the total number of relevant instances. Their formulas are:

$$Precision = \frac{TP}{TP + FP} \tag{9.1}$$

$$Recall = \frac{TP}{TP+FN} \tag{9.2}$$

where TP = True Positive (both the actual as well as predicted class labels are positive), FP = False positive (the predicted class label is positive whereas the actual class label is negative) and FN = False Negative (the predicted class label is negative whereas the actual class label is positive).

The goal is to maximize both of them but if you improve precision, your recall would suffer and vice-versa. There is always a trade-off and which one is more important depends on the problem you are trying to solve. Better precision means less false positives and better recall means less false negatives.

9 **What is a ROC curve? Write pseudo-code to generate the data for such a curve.**

A Receiver Operating Characteristic (ROC) curve plots the True Positive Rate (TPR) vs the False Positive Rate (FPR) as a threshold on the confidence of an instance being positive is varied. A sample ROC curve looks like this:

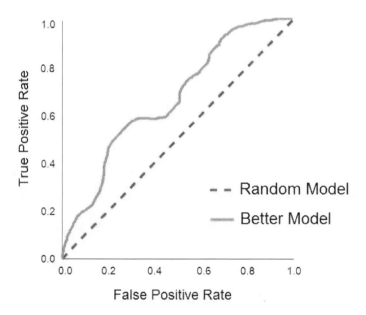

Figure 9.2: ROC curve

The goal, obviously, is to have higher True Positive Rate than False Positive Rate. An algorithm with same TPR and FPR is as good as a random prediction.

Following are the steps to generate a ROC curve:
    (a) Sort the test set predictions according to the confidence that each instance is

positive.

(b) Step through the sorted list from high to low confidence

    i. Locate a threshold between the instances with opposite classes (keeping instances with the same confidence value on the same side of the threshold).

    ii. Compute TPR, FPR for the instances above the threshold.

    iii. Output (FPR, TPR) coordinate on the plot.

10 What is AUROC (AUC)?

AUROC stands for Area Under ROC curve and signifies the probability that a classifier will rank a randomly chosen positive instance higher than a randomly chosen negative one. It is in the range of [0, 1]. The higher the AUROC, the better is the classifier.

11 Why is Area Under ROC Curve (AUROC) better than raw accuracy?

AUROC is robust to class imbalance, unlike raw accuracy. AUROC is constructed using True Positive rate and False Positive rate which are not affected by the class distribution shifting, whereas raw accuracy, based on the class distribution of the test dataset would be affected if the underlying class distribution changes or is unknown.

Let us revisit our Fraud Credit Card Transaction example. You can have a model which always predicts that the transaction is genuine. Since it is mostly true, your model's raw accuracy would be close to 100%. But that's not what you want. You want to have a model with better ability to find a fraud transaction which is achieved by True Positive Rate and False Positive Rate. Hence, AUROC is a better representation of your model's performance.

This page intentionally left blank

10. Natural Language Processing

Natural Language Processing (NLP) is a widely used field within Artificial Intelligence which mainly involves the interactions between the human language and the computer. You can find its applications in a large variety of areas such as Sentiment analysis, Spam detecting, POS (Part-Of-Speech) Tagging, Text summarization, Language translation, Chatbots and so on.

1 **How would you explain NLP to a layman? Why is it difficult to implement?**
NLP stands for Natural Language Processing, the ability of a computer program to understand the human language. It is an extremely challenging field for obvious reasons. NLP requires a computer to understand what humans speak. But, human speech is very often not precise. Humans use slang, pronounce the words differently and can have context in their sentences which is very hard for a computer to process correctly.

2 **What is the use of NLP in Machine Learning?**
At present, NLP is based on Deep Learning. Deep Learning algorithms are a subset of Machine Learning, which need a large amount of data to learn high-level features from data on their own. NLP also works on the same approach and uses deep learning techniques to learn human language and improve upon itself.

3 **What are the different steps in performing Text classification?**
Text classification is a NLP task used to classify the text documents into one or more categories. Classifying whether an email is spam or not, analyzing a person's sentiments from his post, etc. are text classification problems.

A Text classification pipeline involves following steps in order:
(a) Text cleaning
(b) Text annotation to create the features

(c) converting those features into actual predictors

(d) using the predictors to train the model

(e) fine-tune the model to improve its accuracy.

4 What do you understand by Keyword Normalization? Why is it needed?

Keyword normalization, also known as text normalization, is a crucial step in NLP. It is used to transform the keyword into its canonical form, which makes it easier for later processing. It removes stop words such as punctuation marks, words like "a", "an", "the" because these words generally do not carry any weight. After that, it converts the keywords into their standard forms which improves text matching.

For instance, reducing all words to lower cases, converting all tenses to simple present tense. So, if you have "decoration" in one document and "Decorated" in the other, then both of them would be indexed as "decorate". Now, you can easily apply a text matching algorithm on these documents and a query containing a keyword "decorates" would match with both of the documents. Keyword normalization is a very good means of reducing the dimensionality.

5 Tell me about Part-of-speech (POS) tagging.

Part-of-speech tagging is a process of marking the words in a given text as a part of speech such as noun, preposition, adjective, verb etc. It is an extremely challenging task because of its complexity and owing to the fact that the same word could represent a different part of speech in different sentences.

There are generally two techniques used to develop POS tagging algorithms. The first technique is stochastic, which assumes that each word is known and can have a finite set of tags which are learnt during training. And the second technique is rule-based tagging, which uses contextual information to tag each word.

6 Have you heard of the Dependency Parsing algorithm?

Dependency Paring algorithm is a grammar-based text parsing technique which is used for detecting verb phrases, noun phrases, subject and object in the text. "Dependency" implies the relations between the words in a sentence. There are various methods to parse a sentence and analyze its grammatical structure. Some of the common methods include Shift-Reduce and Maximum Spanning Tree.

7 Explain Vector Space Model and its use.

Vector Space Model is an algebraic model which is used to represent an object as a vector of identifiers. Each object (such as a text document) is written as a vector of terms (words) present in it with their weights.

For instance, you have a document "d" with the text "This is an amazing book for the interview preparation."

The corresponding vector for this document is:

$$d = (w_{amazing}, w_{an}, w_{book}, w_{for}, w_{nterview}, w_{is}, w_{preparation}, w_{the}, w_{this})$$

There exist many ways to calculate these weights "w_i". They can be as simple as just the frequency (count) of the words in a document. Similarly, any query is also written in the same fashion. And, the vector operations are used to compare the query with the documents to find the most relevant documents that satisfy the query.

Vector Space Model is used extensively in the fields of Information Retrieval and Indexing. It provides a structure to the unstructured datasets, thereby making it easier to interpret and analyze them.

8 What do you mean by Term Frequency and Inverse Document Frequency?
Term Frequency (tf) is the number of times a *term* occurs in a document divided by the total number of *terms* in that document.

Inverse Document frequency (idf) is a measure of how relevant is the *term* across all the documents. Mathematically, it is the logarithmic of (total number of documents divided by the number of documents containing the *term*).

9 Explain cosine similarity in a simple way.
Cosine similarity captures the similarity between two vectors. As explained in the vector space model, each document and the query is written as a vector of terms.

The cosine is calculated for the query vector with each document, which is normal cosine between two vectors. The resulting cosine value represents the similarity of the document with the given query. If the cosine value is 0 then there is no similarity at all and if it is 1, then the document is the same as the query.

10 Explain N-gram method.
Simply put, an N-gram is a contiguous sequence of n items in the given text. N-gram method is a probabilistic model used to predict an item in a sequence based on the previous n-1 items. You can choose the items to be either the words, phrases etc. If n is 1, then it is called 1-gram, for n = 2, it is 2-gram or bigram and so on.

N-grams can be used for approximate matching. Since they convert the sequence of items into a set of n-grams, you can compare one sequence with another by measuring the percentage of common n-grams in both of them.

11 How many 3-grams can be generated from this sentence "I love New York style pizza"?
Breaking the given sentence into 3-grams, you get:
   (a) I love New
   (b) love New York
   (c) New York style
   (d) York style pizza

```
# We will use CountVectorizer package to demonstrate
```

```
# how to use N-Gram with Scikit-Learn.
# CountVectorizer converts a collection of text documents
# to a matrix of token counts.
# In our case, there is only one document.

from sklearn.feature_extraction.text import CountVectorizer

# N-gram_range specifies the lower and upper boundary on
# the range of N-gram tokens to be extracted.
# For our example, the range is from 3 to 3.
# We have to specify the token_pattern because, by default,
# CountVectorizer treats single character words as stop words

vectorizer = CountVectorizer(ngram_range=(3, 3),
                             token_pattern = r"(?u)\b\w+\b",
                             lowercase=False)

# Now, let's fit the model with our input text
vectorizer.fit(["I love New York style pizza"])

# This will populate vectorizer's vocabulary_
# dictionary with the tokens.
# Let's see the results of this vocabulary
print(vectorizer.vocabulary_.keys())
```

12 Have you heard of the Bag-of-Words model?

The Bag-of-Words model is a very common technique used in Information Retrieval and Natural Language Processing. It is also known as the Vector Space Model, which is described in detail in question 6 above. It uses the frequency of occurrence of the words in a document as the feature value.

One of the limitations of this method is that it does not take into account the order of the words in a document due to which you can not infer the context of the words. For instance, if you take these two sentences "Apple has become a trillion dollar company" and "You should eat apple every day", the Bag-of-Words model won't be able to differentiate between Apple as a company and Apple as a fruit. To address this limitation, you can use N-gram model which stores the spatial information of the words. Bag-of-Words is a special case of N-gram method with n=1.

11. Real World Problems

Almost in every interview, at least one question would be asked on designing a Machine Learning algorithm for a real world problem. This chapter includes most of the system design questions frequently asked in the interviews.

Mostly, the interviewer is interested in your approach towards the problem, how well you understand the problem, and to what extent can you assimilate the intricacies of the system. If you need more details or any clarifications, you should definitely ask the interviewer for it. And always make sure to let your interviewer know of any assumptions that you make in your solution.

The major challenge in preparing for such questions is that there is no "correct" answer. Having prior work experience could be very helpful in answering design related questions since you would have a better understanding of the bottlenecks and trade-offs in using different approaches. But, it certainly does not mean that someone with no experience could not excel.

Following are the major details you need to think about and answer in a system design related question:

- What are the constraints of the system?

- What are the possible use cases of it? How and where would you use such system?

- What is the source and volume of the data? How would you process and store it?

- Do you need to perform any data preprocessing or transformation before applying the algorithm?

- What all features would you extract from the data?

- What kind of problem does it look like? Supervised or Unsupervised?

- What Machine Learning technique would you apply to train your data?

- How do you improve your model's accuracy?

- How can you ensure that your model is correct?

- What are the limitations or bottlenecks of your system and how would you address them?

- How do you handle the scaling issue or time sensitive predictions?

Some of the most frequently asked system design and real life problems are:

1 **Give a common application of Machine Learning that you get to see on a daily basis.**

2 **State some real life problems where Classification algorithms can be used.**

3 **Can you think of some famous scenarios where you would use Clustering algorithm?**

4 **How can a giant company like Amazon detect anomalies in its web services in real-time?**

5 **What is a Recommendation engine? How does it work?**

6 **Design a Recommendation engine.**

7 **How would you do customer recommendation?**

8 **What is Collaborative Filtering?**

9 **What approach would you follow to suggest followers on Twitter?**

10 **How can you find all the images which are a photo of a landscape?**

11 **Design an algorithm for Fraud Detection.**

12 **How would you perform Spam Filtering?**

13 **How would you generate related searches for a search engine?**

14 **How does a search engine work?**

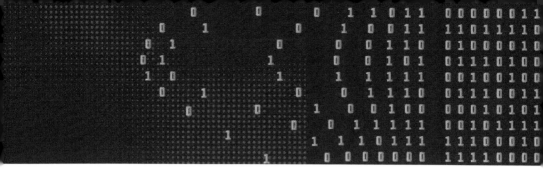

XII. Glossary

Accuracy	The number of correct predictions.
Asymptotic error	The limiting error to which an algorithm converges to ultimately.
Bias	The tendency of the model to underfit or overfit the data.
Categorical variable	A variable which can take one of the limited number of values.
Cluster	It represents a group of objects which are more similar to each other than the objects in another group.
Coefficient	The degree to which changes in the value of one variable impacts the changes in the value of another variable.
Correlation	The extent to which the variables are related to each other.
Covariance	The expected value of the product of the deviations of two variates from their respective expected values.
Covariance matrix	A matrix whose element in the ith row and j^{th} column is the covariance between the ith and j^{th} elements of a random vector.
Cross-validation	A technique to evaluate a Machine Learning model by training and evaluating several models on the subsets of the data.
Data instance	A particular observation of an event.
Degree of freedom	The number of independent variables that can be varied freely to estimate a parameter.
Dimension	Number of attributes or features in the dataset.
Distribution	A function which shows the possible values the data can take and their frequencies.
Entropy	A measure of randomness or uncertainty associated with the data.

Evaluation	A process of measuring the performance of the model.
Feature	An individual attribute or characteristic in the given data.
Feature space	It is the n-dimensions in which the input variables, excluding the target variable, reside.
Global minima	The point whose value is less than the values of all the other points in the domain.
Hyperparameter	Higher-level parameters which define the properties of a model, such as model complexity or learning rate and cannot be learned from the data.
Hyperplane	For an n-dimensional space, it is a subspace of dimension n-1.
Hypersurface	For an n-dimensional space, it is a manifold of dimension n-1.
Hypothesis	A function which is (very close to) the true function that can map input to the output.
Learning rate	A hyper-parameter which signifies how fast does an algorithm converge to its optimal solution.
Linearly separable	When two classes can be split into two half spaces by a hyperplane, they are known as linearly-separable.
Local minima	The point whose value is less than the values of all its neighboring points.
Loss function	The cost incurred by choosing the specific values of the variables.
Misclassification	The number of incorrect predictions.
Model	A specific instance of a Machine Learning algorithm with learned parameters from the input dataset.
Numerical variable	A variable which can take any value within an interval.
Orthogonal	Two variables which are uncorrelated, i.e, independent of each other, are orthogonal to each other.
Overfitting	A condition when the model fits the training dataset to such an extent that it negatively impacts its performance on the test dataset.
Precision	The fraction of values predicted true among all the predicted values.
Predict	Estimate the value of the output variable for a particular data instance.
Recall	The fraction of values predicted true among all the actual true values.
Residual	The difference between the actual value and the predicted value of a data point.

Sparsity	A condition in which most of the entries in the dataset have zero value.
Symmetric matrix	A square matrix which is equivalent to its transpose.
Test dataset	The set of examples used to evaluate the performance of the model.
Time complexity	The amount of time taken by an algorithm to run as a function of the size of its input.
Training dataset	The set of examples used to learn the model, i.e, fit the parameters of the model.
Underfitting	A condition when the model fails to fit both the training as well as the test dataset.
Validation dataset	The set of examples used to evaluate the model in order to tune its hyperparameters.
Variance	A measurement of spread of the values of the data.
Weight	The influence or contribution of a particular variable.

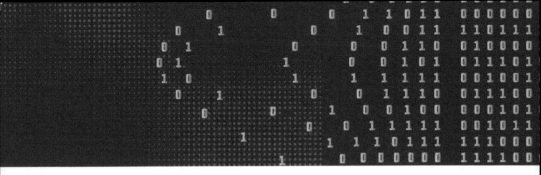

XIII. About The Author

Nitin Suri works as a Software Engineer in the Seller Central group of Amazon, India which provides a worldwide platform for merchants to manage their Marketplace.

Prior to Amazon, Suri was working with Grey Orange Robotics, a startup which designs and manufactures advanced robotics systems. He built various Machine Learning tools, using Predictive Analytics, to predict the delivery and frequency of the shipments and thus, optimize the charging of robots.

Suri is very passionate about robotics, automation and optimization. He has successfully built a Personal File Management System, a file management system for maintaining all the files of a user across various devices. Besides working on interesting algorithm design problems, he is an avid badminton player and also holds a gold medal for winning the Intra College Badminton Championship.

Suri holds a Bachelor's degree in Information Systems from Birla Institute of Technology & Science, Pilani, India and currently resides in Hyderabad, India.